M000113763

HYBRID CHURCH

HYBRID CHURCH

Rethinking the Church for a
Post-Christian Digital Age

JAMES EMERY WHITE

ZONDERVAN
REFLECTIVE

ZONDERVAN REFLECTIVE

Hybrid Church

Copyright © 2023 by James Emery White

Requests for information should be addressed to:
Zondervan, *3900 Sparks Dr. SE, Grand Rapids, Michigan 49546*

Zondervan titles may be purchased in bulk for educational, business, fundraising, or sales promotional use. For information, please email SpecialMarkets@Zondervan.com.

ISBN 978-0-310-14296-6 (hardcover)
ISBN 978-0-310-14298-0 (audio)
ISBN 978-0-310-14297-3 (ebook)

Cover design: Thinkpen Design
Cover art: Shutterstock
Interior design: Sara Colley

Printed in the United States of America

23 24 25 26 27 28 29 30 31 /LSC/ 14 13 12 11 10 9 8 7 6 5 4 3 2 1

Contents

THE NEW, NEW COMMUNITY

A CHURCH FOR THE UNCHURCHED

THINKING STRATEGICALLY

Acknowledgments

I wish to thank the Zondervan team for their support of this project, and specifically acquisitions editor Kyle Rohane for his early enthusiasm for the idea.

Alli Main continues to selflessly serve in the background of every writing endeavor, from books to blogs, patiently editing and fact-checking and, when needed, admonishing. She is a godsend.

To the good folk of Mecklenburg Community Church, who have given me the privilege of serving as senior pastor for more than three decades, I can only express my deepest pride, gratitude, and thanksgiving.

And as always, my wife, Susan, continues to make every page possible, just as she has made every other accomplishment in my life possible.

Introduction

Has the world ever witnessed such change in
so short a time? It to me seems like a dream.
—ELIHU WASHBURNE, NINETEENTH CENTURY[1]

On Wednesday, March 10, 2020, the World Health Organization officially declared that we were in the midst of a pandemic. At that time, there were only thirty-three reported deaths as a result of COVID-19 in the United States. One year later, on Wednesday, March 10, 2021, we were still in a declared state of pandemic with 529,023 deaths having been reported in the US alone. By May 2022, deaths in the US approached one million, and worldwide exceeded five million.[2]

The pandemic did many things to our world beyond the staggering loss of life. Most have been widely reported. That certain sectors of our economy, particularly the travel, restaurant, and entertainment industries, were devastated almost goes without saying. In education, despite dedicated educators' noble efforts to engage students, it was a year fraught with challenges, with many students falling behind. And as an article in the *New York Times* noted, many have experienced a "childhood without children"—a year or more of their lives without birthday parties, playdates, and daycare. There is almost universal affirmation that our political culture, social discourse, and social interactions have degraded tremendously. You will find the occasional person who believes the pandemic brought out the best in society, expressing an appreciation for the government's response to the pandemic, commenting on the kindness of strangers, or recognizing the reduction in traffic or pollution. "However," as a Pew Research Center report on the effects of the COVID-19 pandemic noted, "these kinds of responses were so rare that researchers were unable to reliably measure them."[3]

These are not short-term impacts.

But few areas of our collective experience were more profoundly affected than our religious lives, and particularly our gathered religious communities. It wasn't simply that most churches were closed for significant lengths of time or that financial challenges related to diminished giving reared their heads or that upon reopening most found their in-person attendance significantly lower than before.[4] We were also beset with pastoral burnout, the moral failure of noteworthy leaders, and widespread spiritual fatigue. Yet in the midst of that darkness shone a light: that a larger narrative—growing larger with hindsight—is the incredible opportunity the pandemic gave the Western church to transition to the model it desperately needed to be transitioning to in the first place.

Early in the pandemic, I wrote that I began to see signs that the pandemic just might be the catalyst needed to turn around a declining church. What if the path most churches were on, if not forced into a radical redirection, would have guaranteed their continued marginalization, irrelevance, and decline? What if the pandemic was forcing countless churches to change in ways that would actually allow them to grow in both size and influence?

It was true. The pandemic, early on, positively altered the church in at least five desperately needed ways.

First, churches were forced to move from a weekend-only crowd-centric approach to a seven-day-a-week incarnational approach. While every church should promote corporate worship, too many churches made that celebration the be-all and end-all of the life of the church. We say that the church isn't bricks and mortar but rather a community of faith that can be strategically served by bricks and mortar, yet too many churches were never leaving the building.[5] The church is to be in the community where it resides, attempting to reach out and serve in the name of Jesus. Early on, the pandemic broke us out of our gospel ghettos and holy huddles and into the neighborhoods and streets where we live, particularly as individual Christians. We weren't able to gather as a community of faith, but we were able to walk our neighborhoods and meet people we had never met before.

Second, churches were forced online. You would think that the vast majority of churches already would have been online. They weren't.[6] I don't mean they didn't have a website—most did. I mean they didn't have an online presence. Prior to the pandemic, a relatively small fraction of Protestant churches in the technologically advanced US, much less in the wider world, had an online campus or had ever streamed a service on Facebook. But virtually overnight, the vast majority of churches *did* have an online presence.[7] Churches were finally going where the world actually lived.

Third, churches were forced to embrace social media. Before the pandemic, most churches not only did not have an online presence but also did not embrace or use social media. A study found that prepandemic, only 15 percent of churches in the US were using Twitter or Instagram.[8] Yet, as churches quickly learned, social media is the communication network of the modern world. Increasingly it's how people relate, get their news, and interact with organizations. The pandemic forced churches to learn to communicate the way the people they were trying to reach were communicating.

Fourth, churches were forced to innovate and change. Necessity, it has been said, is the mother of invention. It is also the mother of change. When you are forced to stop doing things the way you have always done them and must find a way to soldier on, you are pushed into new ways of thinking and acting. Some have opined that the seven last words of a dying church are, "We've never done it that way before." In the nick of time, at least for many churches, churches were having to say, "We must do things like never before." That takes a church from seven words before death to seven words before life.

Finally, churches were brought back to mission. When all your ways of doing things are stripped away, you are left with something raw and unfiltered: your real reason to exist. When faced with, say, the inability to meet for a Sunday service, you are forced to ask yourself what you were trying to do through that Sunday service and then go about doing it.

Then, just as we had found our footing, just as we were making inroads we'd never made before, at our first opportunity, we went right back to business as usual. Don't get me wrong, there was nothing but joy in once again offering in-person services, but I can't begin to tell you how many pastors and church leaders I heard express that the key to everything being well again was the ability to meet again. They said they hoped they would never hear the phrase "Facebook streaming" again for the rest of their lives.

But then came the shock: people didn't return in droves. The reason had little to do with the pandemic, which only provided the smokescreen. Churches have been seeing declining attendance for some time. The pandemic accelerated and widened the effect of two profound

> ## FIVE WAYS THE PANDEMIC INITIALLY TURNED THE CHURCH
>
> 1. Churches were forced to move from a weekend-only crowd-centric approach to a seven-day-a-week incarnational approach.
> 2. Churches were forced online.
> 3. Churches were forced to embrace social media.
> 4. Churches were forced to innovate and change.
> 5. Churches were brought back to mission.

cultural changes that hold enormous import for the life and mission of the church: the new reality of a post-Christian world and the digital revolution.

In his book *Think Again*, Adam Grant writes of three prevailing mindsets: that of the preacher, the prosecutor, and the politician. With each we take on a particular identity and use a distinct set of tools. If our closely held beliefs are challenged, we go into preacher mode and deliver "sermons" to protect or promote our beliefs. If we recognize flaws in another person's reasoning, we go into prosecutor mode and marshal arguments to prove them wrong and make our case. If the goal is to win over an audience, we go into politician mode and campaign for approval. "The risk," writes Grant, "is that we become so wrapped up in preaching that we're right, prosecuting others who are wrong, and politicking for support that we don't bother to rethink our own views."[9]

Grant argues for a fourth mindset: that of the scientist. "If you're a scientist by trade, rethinking is fundamental to your profession. You're paid to be constantly aware of the limits of your understanding. You're expected to doubt what you know, be curious about what you don't know, and update your views based on new data."[10] But being a scientist, Grant points out, is not just a profession, it's a frame of mind. It is a "mode of thinking that differs from preaching, prosecuting, and politicking."[11]

I hope that Grant's use of *preaching* in a semi-pejorative way and his highlighting of a scientist in a favorable way don't figure so literally in your mind that you want to defend the role of sermons and lambast the secular scientific mind and thus fail to get his larger point. He's making the case for the necessary rethinking that too often is thwarted by resistant mindsets. For example, he lists the four most annoying things people say instead of rethinking:[12]

"That will never work here."

"That's not what my experience has shown."

"That's too complicated; let's not overthink it."
"That's the way we've always done it."

If you have ever caught yourself saying or thinking any of those sentences, you need to do some rethinking. I hope you will allow me to ask you to think about a simple assertion, even if you end up disagreeing with it in the end: we must rethink the church's approach to fulfilling its mission in a post-Christian, digital age. That rethinking hinges on a single word: hybrid. The church must bring together the physical and the digital, and it must be a vibrant community of faith for churchgoers as well as a church for the unchurched. These twin dynamics are at the heart of the new hybrid model.

Before we begin our exploration, it would be helpful for you to know that I write with my feet planted in two worlds. The first is a scholarly world. I write as a former seminary president and current professor of theology and culture. The second is a ministry world. I write as the founding and senior pastor of Mecklenburg Community Church (Meck), which experiences more than 70 percent of its growth from the unchurched. The convergence of these two worlds has fueled much of my reflection and writing, not to mention my work as a scholar and pastor. I would argue it has made my work better. It's difficult as a pastor to read someone who has never pastored tell me how to lead and guide and build a church. It's even more difficult when that person tells me how the church should respond to changing cultural tides—critiquing a church for, say, being online when that is where this person lives and promotes themselves. It is equally difficult to read a church practitioner who shows little understanding of the difference between being in the world and of the world, or of the enormous challenges—even dangers—inherent in front-lines engagement with a post-Christian world on its own turf. An old proverb bears repeating when you attempt to reach into a lost world for its redemption: if you are going to dine with the devil, you best bring a long spoon.[13] Too many practitioners act as if they are not even sitting at the table.

This book has two major sections. The first (chaps. 1–6) outlines the dynamics and depth of the two new realities. Following an interlude that argues for a new approach and model are a series of chapters (7–17) on the four major rethinkings: the centrality of the internet, a revisioning of community, becoming a church for the unchurched, and how we must become strategic in all our thinking.

—Ad Majorem Dei Gloriam

OUR
POST-CHRISTIAN
WORLD

From Christian to Post-Christian

We are not in Christianity, not anymore.

—POPE FRANCIS¹

For the first time in human history, the majority of the West now live in a post-Christian world. I say the first time because there have been only three eras in relation to the Christian faith: pre-Christian, Christian, and now post-Christian. Only when you understand how Christian the culture of the West has been can you see how post-Christian it has become.²

THE CHRISTIAN WORLD

The beginning of the era of the "Christian world" is often associated with the conversion of Roman Emperor Constantine in 310. The era was, ironically, cemented with the sacking of Rome in 410 by the barbarian

Alaric and the beginning of the Middle Ages, which left the church the sole remaining institution capable of providing social glue.

During the medieval era, which historian Marcia Colish has argued is the beginning of the history of Western culture as we have known it, it was a Christian world.[3] As Johan Huizinga contended, the "life of medieval Christendom is permeated in all aspects by religious images. There is nothing and no action that is not put in its relationship to Christ and faith."[4] Or as medieval historian Norman Cantor put it, "Medieval culture was a culture of the Book, and in the Middle Ages, the Book was the Bible."[5]

To be sure, the religious beliefs of the common people were somewhat less refined than those of educated churchmen, often involving a mixture of pagan thinking and Christian philosophy, yet a common understanding of the world was firmly in place on a Christian foundation. Jeffrey Burton Russell writes that a "sacred, rather than a profane, view of the world was generally assumed. Everything was created by God, and, as God was immanent in the world, everything was an expression of God."[6]

Eventually a deeply entrenched awareness and acceptance of God developed into a full-blown idea of a Christian society, and "Christendom" was born. Following the edict of Emperor Theodosius in 380 mandating that all under his rule profess Christianity, according to Martin Marty, "the question was no longer whether society would be Christian, but rather how this was to be realized."[7] It all culminated on Christmas Day in 800 when Pope Leo III crowned Charlemagne as emperor with the titles that had been reserved for the Roman rulers of the past.

Though Europe quickly descended into a feudal society and became littered with papal and imperial conflict, for the next eight hundred or more years, the politics, learning, social organization, art, music, economics, and law of Europe was Christian, though not in the sense of fully incorporating the values of the Christian faith—no one should romanticize the spiritual piety of the individual or community during this time. Indeed, it was the worldliness of the institutional church toward the end of the Middle Ages that helped incite the Reformation. Yet we should not trivialize as merely political the Christian nature of self and society.[8] No matter the back and forth between pope and emperor, between church and state, it never entered anyone's mind to establish a secular society.

This medieval synthesis, as it has sometimes been called, brought together the secular and the sacred spheres of life. Historian Mark Noll writes that it was an "integrated view of life in which everything— politics, social order, religious practice, economic relationships, and more—was based on the Christian faith . . . and protected by the actions of secular rulers."[9] The vision for all was for a Christian society, and to live and act and think Christianly within it.

Contrary to common belief, this vision didn't end with the Renaissance and the transition from the medieval to the modern world, much less with the onset of what has been termed *humanism*. As the name implies, humanism was largely a celebration of the humanities and humanity itself. Initially, humanism neither involved nor demanded an undermining of the Christian worldview that had been established during the medieval era. One could argue instead that humanism invigorated it, for the learning was taking place within a Christian context. Social historian Fernand Braudel referred to the early humanism of the Renaissance as a robust and complimentary "dialogue of Rome with Rome," meaning between pagan Rome and Christian Rome, between classical and Christian civilization.[10] So while the early humanism of the Renaissance was built around a return to things classical, it was in light of a belief in a creator. It was a Christian, or sacred, humanism. Despite some bumps along the road, the early humanism of the Renaissance was actually a call for a richer and more rounded Christian culture.[11] It was religious and if anything was concerned with the renewal rather than the eradication of the Christian church.[12]

Only when humanism was ripped from its Christian moorings and became a secular humanism did the interplay between Renaissance humanism and Christianity become adversarial. When humanism became, to use Francis Schaeffer's descriptive, "autonomous"—divorced from the anchor of biblical revelation and a Christian worldview—it became destructive.[13] Others would say humanism became enlightened, and thus the era known as the Enlightenment was born. But it took a few more centuries for the transition from the Christian world to the post-Christian world to take effect.

But take effect it did.

THE POST-CHRISTIAN WORLD

Today, the distant echoes of the medieval culture upon which the West was built can barely be heard. As sociologist Christian Smith notes, "Something real at the level of macrosocial change . . . has actually happened in history."[14] The earliest manifestation of this seismic shift was the French Revolution, which established a religion of man. A process of de-Christianization began, so much so that Alexis de Tocqueville later wrote that "in France . . . Christianity was attacked with almost frenzied violence."[15] One of the more symbolic events took place on November 10, 1793, when Cathedrale Notre-Dame de Paris, the great church of France and most famous of the Gothic cathedrals, whose foundation stone was laid by Pope Alexander III in 1163, was formally declared to be and transformed into the Temple of Reason, with busts of Rousseau and Voltaire taking the place of the saints. During the ceremony, a hymn to Liberty was sung:

> Descend, O Liberty, daughter of Nature;
> The people have recaptured their immortal power:
> Over the pompous remains of age-old imposture

Their hands raise thine altar. . . .

Thou, holy Liberty, come dwell in this temple

Be the goddess of the French.[16]

But the post-Christian nature of the Western world has not been widely understood, even as late as the twentieth century. One reason is that while the subculture that rested at the top of the epicenters of society—the educational system, the media of mass communication, and the upper echelons of the legal system—had been largely secularized, late sociologist Peter Berger argued rightly that the world was "as furiously religious as it ever was, and in some places more so than ever."[17] He even famously quipped, "If India is the most religious country on our planet, and Sweden is the least religious, America is a land of Indians ruled by Swedes."[18]

At the time, he was right. But times have changed. Now we are keenly feeling the post-Christian nature of our world, and not simply at the top of cultural epicenters. We are, to borrow from Berger, increasingly a land of Swedes.

THE MARKS OF A POST-CHRISTIAN MINDSET

So what defines a post-Christian mindset?[19] There are four marks: moral relativism, autonomous individualism, narcissistic hedonism, and reductive naturalism.[20]

MORAL RELATIVISM

The basic idea of moral relativism is that "what is true for you is true for you, and what is true for me is true for me." What is moral is dictated by a particular situation in a particular culture or social location. Few books championed this value more directly than Joseph Fletcher's *Situation Ethics*. Fletcher challenged the role of rules in the making of moral decisions, maintaining that one must determine in each and every situation what the most appropriate thing to do is. If it is determined that what is appropriate demands the suspension of established rules, so be it. Moral values are a matter of personal opinion or private judgment rather than grounded in objective truth. This idea was so entrenched by the late 1980s that Allan Bloom, reflecting on his role as a university educator, maintained that there "is one thing a professor can be absolutely certain of. Almost every student entering the university believes, or says he believes, that truth is relative."[21] Of course, the nature of moral relativism in our day is that what is considered to be moral is based not on anything transcendent but on our individual sense of choice.

AUTONOMOUS INDIVIDUALISM

"Man is the being whose project is to be God."[22] This penetrating assessment, offered by French existentialist philosopher Jean-Paul Sartre, is particularly accurate of modern man. In reviewing the past five hundred years of Western cultural life, Jacques Barzun concluded that one of the great themes is emancipation, the desire for independence from all authority. Barzun concludes that for the modern era, it is perhaps the most characteristic cultural theme of all.[23] The value of autonomous individualism maintains that each person is independent in terms of destiny and accountability. Ultimate moral authority is self-generated. In the end, we answer to no one but ourselves, for we are truly on our own. Our choices are ours alone, determined by personal pleasure and not by any higher moral authority. Intriguingly, Thomas Oden noted that this is the force behind the idea of heresy. The "key to 'hairesis' (root word for 'heresy') is the notion of choice—choosing for *oneself*, over against the apostolic tradition."[24]

It was during the Reformation that the individualism of the modern world took root. The Reformation made the pursuit and practice of faith a matter of personal responsibility. The will of God was to be determined individually and then followed. But by the second half of the nineteenth century this individualism morphed into the idea of having the right to do whatever you wanted provided it did not harm others. After the Second World War, Steve Bruce notes, the idea of individualism shifted yet again, even to the point of changing the scope of the question. "We claim not only the right to do what is right in our own eyes but to assert that the world is as we variously see it."[25] Within autonomous individualism are the seeds for the presumption that would seek to cast God from his throne and assert humanity in his place as the conduit of divine power.

> **FOUR MARKS OF THE POST-CHRISTIAN MIND**
>
> 1. Moral Relativism
> 2. Autonomous Individualism
> 3. Narcissistic Hedonism
> 4. Reductive Naturalism

And we have wasted little time.

On July 25, 2003, the first test-tube baby turned twenty-five. Robert Edwards, who along with his partner, Patrick Steptoe, pioneered the procedure, graced the occasion with a rare but candid interview with the *Times* of London. "It was a fantastic achievement but it was about more than infertility," said Edwards, then seventy-seven and emeritus professor of human reproduction at Cambridge University. "I wanted to find out exactly who was in charge, whether it was God himself or whether it was scientists in the laboratory."

Smiling triumphantly at the reporter, he said, "It was us."[26]

NARCISSISTIC HEDONISM

In Greek mythology, Narcissus is the character who, upon passing his reflection in the water, becomes so enamored with himself that he devotes the rest of his life to his own reflection. From this we get our term *narcissism*, the preoccupation with self.

The value of narcissistic hedonism is the "I, me, mine" mentality that places personal pleasure and fulfillment at the forefront of concerns. Or as Francis Schaeffer maintained throughout his writings, the ultimate ethic of our day is the pursuit of personal peace and individual affluence. Whether knowingly or not, noted cultural historian Christopher Lasch agreed with Schaeffer's assessment and christened ours "the culture of narcissism," determining that the current taste is for individual therapy instead of religion. The quest for personal well-being, health, and psychic security has replaced the older hunger for personal salvation.[27] This runs deeper than mere self-gratification. Narcissism has become a guiding worldview. Stanley Grenz observed that Anselm's famed dictum "I believe in order that I may understand" was altered by the Enlightenment to become "I believe what I can understand."[28] The modern twist goes farther, becoming "I believe when I understand that it helps me." Today, narcissistic behavior is hardly noticed. In a time when "flaunting your best self on social media has become a norm, narcissistic traits seem to be everywhere."[29]

REDUCTIVE NATURALISM

Gerard Piel, founder and publisher of *Scientific American* magazine, argued that when historians examine twentieth-century Western civilization, it will be deemed the "age of science." Not only have the practical details of daily life been transformed by scientific advances but the sense of who we are, how our world came to be, our role in it, our origin, and even our ultimate fate have been influenced by scientific thinking as never before in human history.[30]

But in terms of the world that lives in us, this elevation of science has taken a particular turn. For example, Berger suggests that the influence of secularization can be most clearly seen "in the rise of science as an autonomous, thoroughly secular perspective on the world."[31] Scientist Ian Barbour offers a firsthand analysis. Mirroring the historical trail from the Renaissance to the Enlightenment, he writes that when religion first met modern science in the seventeenth century, the encounter was a friendly one. "By the eighteenth century many scientists believe in a God who had designed the universe, but they no longer believe in a personal God actively involved in the world and human life. By the nineteenth century," Barbour concludes, ". . . scientists were hostile to religion."[32]

That hostility is rooted in what can be called reductive naturalism. Naturalism is the idea that nature is all that is. Reductive naturalism is the value that states that all that can be known within nature is that which can be empirically verified. So reductive naturalism contends that what is real is only that which can be seen, tasted, heard, smelled, or touched, then verified—able to be replicated in a test tube. Knowledge is reduced to this level of knowing. If it cannot be examined in a tangible, scientific manner, it is not simply unknowable, it is meaningless.[33]

This naturalism holds that life is accidental. There is nothing beyond us that will ever bring order, reason, or explanation. We must restrict what can be known to what is immediately before us, to what is given or factual—what can be empirically or scientifically demonstrated. As astronomer Carl Sagan argued in his final work, the goal is to rid ourselves of a "demon-haunted" world, meaning anything that challenges the rule of science and technology as the ultimate arbiter of truth and reality, for there is no other truth or reality to embrace.[34] So we have not simply science but scientism—the deification of scientific methods and results as religion. As will be seen, however, this does not mean that people will not search for the transcendent outside of the realms of science, specifically the world of the occult.

The trauma of our world is that moral relativism has led to a crisis in values; we find ourselves needing them but not having them, and divorced from any means of finding them. Autonomous individualism has led to a lack of vision; there is nothing calling us upward to be more than we are beyond ourselves. Narcissistic hedonism has fostered empty souls;

anyone who has followed its ever-deadening trail knows how hollow its entreaties are. Reductive naturalism has proven inadequate for human experience; we intuitively know that there is more to reality than what our five senses can determine.

This inability for life to actually work apart from God was seen by many from the beginning. Voltaire himself refused to let men talk atheism in front of the maids. "I want my lawyer, tailor, valets, even my wife, to believe in God; I think that if they do I shall be robbed less and cheated less."[35] Such sentiments led historian Christopher Dawson to the central thesis of his life's work: not simply that you cannot study culture apart from religion but that culture cannot survive without religion. "The society of culture which has lost its spiritual roots is a dying culture," he declared, "however prosperous it may appear externally."[36]

This is the world's great quandary.

We are plagued not by the first part of Nietzsche's famous claim that "God is dead" but increasingly by his second, less well-known assertion that "we have killed him." From this comes the true challenge of the modern world: "How shall we, the murderer of all murderers, comfort ourselves?"[37]

The Rise of the Nones

The explosion of people with no religion
will be a huge story in this century.
—DAN GILGOFF, FORMER RELIGION EDITOR, CNN[1]

I have long contended that the most significant religious trend of our lifetimes is the rise of the "nones." As I wrote in my book *The Rise of the Nones*, the nones are the religiously unaffiliated. When asked in various surveys and polls about their religion or faith affiliation, they do not answer Baptist or Catholic or any other defined faith. They simply say "I'm nothing" or check "none."

When I began researching and writing about the nones, they were one out of every five Americans, which made them the second largest religious group in the United States—second only to Catholics.[2] Not only that, but they were also the fastest growing religious group in the nation. In 2021, the percentage of Americans who self-designated as atheist, agnostic, or of no particular faith rose to 29 percent of all US adults (fig. 2.1). That is nearly one out of every three adults, up ten percentage points from when surveyed in 2011. The same survey found that the number of professing Christians dropped from 75 percent in 2011 to 63 percent in 2021. Digging further, Pew found that during the same ten-year period, those who prayed daily dropped thirteen percentage points, and the number who said religion was important to their lives dropped fifteen. The conclusion of the Pew researchers was fitting: "The secularizing shifts evident in American society so far in the twenty-first century show no signs of slowing. . . . The religiously unaffiliated share of the public is six percentage points higher than it was five years ago and ten points higher than a decade ago."[3]

The rise in the number of the unaffilated from just around 5 percent in the 1940s to 29 percent now makes it clear we are experiencing a vast cultural realignment. Even more stunning is that when you set apart those who are between the ages of eighteen to twenty-nine, the youngest of those surveyed, the self-designation marks 39 percent.[4] When you chart the rise of the nones even from just 1972 to 2016, the increase is extraordinary (fig. 2.2).

These changes are reflected in church membership. According to a Gallup survey, Americans' membership in houses of worship has continued to decline to such a degree that it has now dropped below 50 percent for the first time in Gallup's eight-decade trend. In 2020, only 47 percent of Americans said they belonged to a church, synagogue, or mosque, down from 50 percent in 2018 and 70 percent in 1999. As anyone in the social sciences will tell you, that precipitous of a drop in such a short period is simply jaw dropping.

As might be expected when analyzing the shift according to generations, the younger you are, the more likely you are to be unchurched. Among those Gallup calls traditionalists, meaning those born before 1946, 66 percent belong to a church. Among baby boomers, the number drops to 58 percent, and the number plummets to only 36 percent among millennials. Early data on Generation Z suggests the percentage of involvement is at least as low (if not lower than) millennials.

FIGURE 2.1
Pew Research Center

In U.S., roughly three-in-ten adults now religiously unaffiliated

% of U.S. adults who identify with ...

78% 63%
Christianity

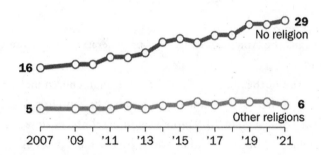

29
No religion

16 ....

5 6
Other religions

2007 '09 '11 '13 '15 '17 '19 '21

Note: Those who did not answer are not shown.
Source: Data from 2020-21 based on Pew Research Center's
National Public Opinion Reference Surveys (NPORS), conducted
online and by mail among a nationally representative group of
respondents recruited using address-based sampling. All data from
2019 and earlier from the Center's random-digit-dial telephone
surveys, including the 2007 and 2014 Religious Landscape Studies.
See Methodology for details.
"About Three-in-Ten U.S. Adults Are Now Religiously Unaffiliated"

PEW RESEARCH CENTER

FIGURE 2.2
PRRI

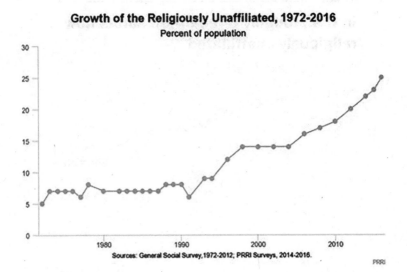

Growth of the Religiously Unaffiliated, 1972-2016
Percent of population

Sources: General Social Survey,1972-2012; PRRI Surveys, 2014-2016.

PRRI

This means the American church is one generation away from being devastated.[5]

The rise of the nones and the drop in overall church membership have also resulted in a decline in the number of churches. According to Lifeway Research, in 2019 more Protestant churches closed (4,500) than opened (3,000).[6] Another study, by the Center for Analytics, Research and Data, found an even higher rate of closures, estimating that in the decade ending in 2020, 3,850 to 7,700 houses of worship closed each year in the United States. That's between seventy-five and 150 congregations each week.[7] This, of course, was before the pandemic's effect, which accelerated closings among churches that were already on life support.

It's even worse in the UK. According to the National Centre for Social Research, more than 50 percent identify as a none, and another 10 percent subscribe to a non-Christian religion. Two-thirds of people in

Britain never attend religious services. The portion of the British population identifying as Christian has fallen from two-thirds (66 percent) to just over one-third (38 percent) since 1983. Or to put it another way, the self-described religious outnumbered the nonreligious by 38 percent to 28 percent in 1998, but now the nonreligious are 44 percent and the religious only 31 percent. Now only half of people claim to ever pray (49 percent).[8] The Office for National Statistics has found that atheists now account for more than a third of "faith" groups.[9]

Consider Ireland. As a *Washington Post* article noted, "Once the most Catholic country in Europe, Ireland is now a place where only about a third of adults attend church weekly." Though Ireland is a country once known for its Catholic conservatism, Ireland's courts and legislature have recently overturned bans on contraception, homosexuality, and divorce. As Crawford Gibbon, professor of history at Queen's University Belfast noted, it all goes to "illustrate how rapid Irish secularization has been—it has achieved in one generation what took centuries elsewhere."[10]

Ireland is part of a larger shift throughout Western Europe. As a recent Pew Research Center report detailed, the "majority of Europe's Christians are nonpracticing."[11] Only 22 percent attend church services. That among still-professing Christians the vast majority are nonpracticing reveals this is the last generation of any significant cohort of professing Christians, because the state of being a nonpracticing Christian is surely the final step before not professing any allegiance at all. In most Western European countries, nonpracticing Christians are the largest group (fig. 2.3). Note in figure 2.3 the comparisons between those who consider themselves nonpracticing Christians and those who are practicing Christians. Since the time of that study, things have worsened. In France, recent surveys have discovered that the majority of the population—yes, the majority—are now atheists.[12]

So while Christianity remains the world's largest faith and is even on the rise in the Global South, it is no longer the dominant cultural

FIGURE 2.3
Pew Research Center

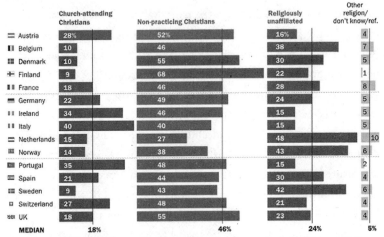

In most Western European countries, non-practicing Christians are largest group
% who are ...

	Church-attending Christians	Non-practicing Christians	Religiously unaffiliated	Other religion/ don't know/ref.
Austria	28%	52%	16%	4
Belgium	10	46	38	7
Denmark	10	55	30	5
Finland	9	68	22	1
France	18	46	28	8
Germany	22	49	24	5
Ireland	34	46	15	5
Italy	40	40	15	5
Netherlands	15	27	48	10
Norway	14	38	43	6
Portugal	35	48	15	2
Spain	21	44	30	4
Sweden	9	43	42	6
Switzerland	27	48	21	4
UK	18	55	23	4
MEDIAN	**18%**	**46%**	**24%**	**5%**

Note: Church-attending Christians are defined as those who say they attend church at least monthly. Non-practicing Christians are defined as those who attend less often. Other religion/don't know/ref. are mostly Muslim respondents. General population surveys in Western Europe may not fully capture the size of minority populations, such as Muslims. Therefore, these figures may differ from previously published demographic estimates. Figures may not add to 100% due to rounding.
Source: Survey conducted April–August 2017 in 15 countries. See Methodology for details.
"Being Christian in Western Europe"

PEW RESEARCH CENTER

force in the West. Nor do those in the West want it to be. Recent surveys find that Americans' confidence in the church is in a freefall. Currently, only 36 percent have confidence in any aspect of organized religion, a new low since charting began in 1974.[13]

It is important to note that, France notwithstanding, the rise of the nones and the decline in church attendance and membership is not the same as a decline in belief in God. Indeed, in places like the United States, the overwhelming majority are theists. Research has found that even among the nones, only 21 percent said their self-designation as a none was because they didn't believe in God. The most common reason offered was that they simply questioned various religious teachings (fig. 2.4).[14]

You can think of it this way: we have a world full of people who are open to and even believe in God but reject religious pathways to that God, religious dogma about that God, and religious groups adhering to that God. The verdict is in: God, yes. Religion, no.

FIGURE 2.4
Pew Research Center

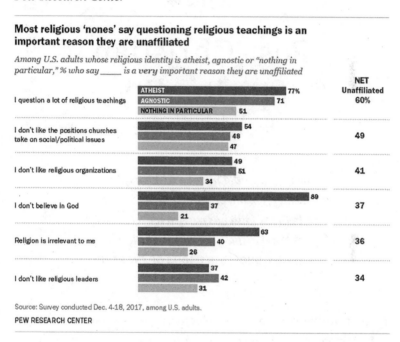

Most religious 'nones' say questioning religious teachings is an important reason they are unaffiliated

Among U.S. adults whose religious identity is atheist, agnostic or "nothing in particular," % who say _____ is a very important reason they are unaffiliated

		NET Unaffiliated
I question a lot of religious teachings	ATHEIST 77% AGNOSTIC 71 NOTHING IN PARTICULAR 51	60%
I don't like the positions churches take on social/political issues	54 48 47	49
I don't like religious organizations	49 51 34	41
I don't believe in God	89 37 21	37
Religion is irrelevant to me	63 40 26	36
I don't like religious leaders	37 42 31	34

Source: Survey conducted Dec. 4-18, 2017, among U.S. adults.
PEW RESEARCH CENTER

Post-Christian Spirituality

I believe in God. I'm not a religious fanatic.
I can't remember the last time I went to
church. My faith has carried me a long way.
It's "Sheilaism." Just my own little voice.

—SHEILA, QUOTED IN *HABITS OF THE HEART*[1]

So where have the nones gone? Not to another religious brand, per se. It is more accurate to say they have adopted different approaches to spirituality than a defined religion. As Ross Douthat notes, Christianity is being replaced not by atheism but by "post-Christian spiritualities— pantheist, gnostic, syncretist, pagan."[2] Or as an article in the *New York Times* put it, "When did everybody become a witch?"[3] Because of the vast number of new witch books that came out in the fall of 2019 alone, *Publishers Weekly* declared it the "season of the witch."[4] As one study found, there may now be more Americans who identify as practicing witches than there are members of mainline Presbyterianism in the US.[5]

It doesn't help that the spiritual soil is perfect for a warm embrace and cultural mainstreaming of all things witchcraft. Most Americans "mix traditional faith with beliefs in psychics, reincarnation and spiritual energy that they say can be found in physical objects such as mountains, trees and crystals."[6] A staggering 41 percent of Americans believe in psychics. A stunning 42 percent believe spiritual energy can be located in physical objects.[7] It should be noted that the younger the demographic, the more pronounced this trend becomes. Consider Generation Z's embrace of tarot cards. As Heather Greene notes in a Religion News Service article, "Generation Z has been the driving force behind the renewed popularity and mainstreaming of the age-old esoteric system. As Theresa Reed, known online as the Tarot Lady, put it, 'It's not just for witches anymore.'"[8]

This spiritualism isn't limited to the occult. More than half of American adults and more than 75 percent of younger Americans believe in intelligent extraterrestrial life, rivaling the level of belief in God.[9] And not just belief in intelligent extraterrestrial life but religious philosophies based on said life. Consider "Jedism," a religion based on the philosophy of the Jedi characters in Star Wars media.[10] George Lucas once quipped, upon the release of a Star Wars movie, "Well, it's not a religious event. I hate to tell people that. It's a movie, just a movie." Yes, but commenting on Lucas's statement, D. W. Pasulka aptly titled a chapter in her book on UFOs, religion, and technology, "When Star Wars Became Real."[11] Because culturally, and spiritually for many, it did.

But there is something even more new and disturbing in regard to post-Christian spirituality, particularly among the youngest of generations. It has been called a type of "new cult" or a "TikTok spirituality."[12] A *Vox* article calls it a new kind of religion forming on the internet, stating that "algorithms are surfacing content that combines Christian ideas like prosperity gospel with New Age and non-Western spirituality—along with some conspiracy theories."[13] Rebecca Jennings, a journalist at *Vox* who covers internet culture, adds that "part of the draw of internet spirituality is that it's perfectly pick-and-choosable—but more than anything, they believe in the importance of keeping an open mind to whatever else might be out there."[14] When she asked Joseph Russo, a professor of anthropology at Wesleyan University, whether this loosely related web of beliefs could ever come together to form in its own kind of religion, he replied, "I think it already has."[15] Jennings' description is telling:

> Call it the religion of "just asking questions." Or the religion of "doing your own research." It's still in its infancy and has evolved in an attempt to correct a societal wrong: that the world is a pretty f***ed up place and it doesn't seem like the current system of dealing with it is really working, so maybe something else is going on, something just out of reason's reach. The religion of the internet has also already culminated in real-world violence, the most obvious examples being the QAnon-related coup on January 6 and the conspiracy theories surrounding lifesaving vaccines. Yet its more innocuous effects have been likewise transformative.
>
> Consider the widespread mainstreaming of astrology over the past decade, the renewed interest in holistic medicine, or the girl-boss optimism of multilevel marketing companies. These are all frameworks of belief that question traditional logic and institutional thought—for instance, that science-backed medicinal practices work better to cure disease than essential oils, that 99 percent of people who sign up for an MLM end up losing money, or that the idea that your entire personality can be determined by the positioning of the stars at the time of your birth is fundamentally false. . . .
>
> The religion of the internet posits questions like, "what's the harm in believing?" and "why shouldn't I be prepared for the worst?" The deeper you go, the harder those questions are to answer.[16]

I am taken with Steve Smith's argument that our challenge is not between faith and secularism but between two different religious faiths, paralleling the cultural challenge of the early church and Rome.[17] As Peter Leithart wrote of Smith's thesis, "The Romans were pragmatic and worldly, yet they believed their greatest strength was devotion to the empire's gods. . . . The paganism of Rome treated the world as sacred. But Christianity introduced a radically different perspective. Christians—while affirming the world's goodness—located the sacred in another world altogether. In other words, paganism was an immanent form of religiosity, while Christianity embraced the transcendent."[18]

Or even more to the point, we "don't have a naked public square. We have a pagan public square from which transcendent appeals and symbols, even implicit ones, are excluded."[19]

POST-CHRISTIAN MORALITY

What we're seeing is not simply a changing spirituality but also, as one would assume, a changing morality. The Gallup organization conducts an annual poll on American values and beliefs. From a list of twenty-one behaviors, they rank what is currently considered morally acceptable and morally wrong. Currently, the three most morally acceptable behaviors are birth control, drinking alcohol, and getting a divorce. The least acceptable behaviors are extramarital affairs, cloning humans, suicide, and polygamy.[20]

What is most disturbing are the comparisons. More people think that buying or wearing clothing made of animal fur is morally wrong than think that doctor-assisted suicide (euthanasia) is wrong. The list also gives insight into what we think makes something immoral. The most reprehensible behavior on the list was having an extramarital affair. Yet the poll also found that sex between an unmarried man and woman, having a baby outside of marriage, and gay or lesbian relations were morally acceptable. In regard to sexual behavior, only sex between teenagers, pornography, polygamy, and married men and women having an affair were felt to be wrong.[21] Similar findings were made when a study of a like kind was performed in the UK.[22]

But the larger point is clear. We are living in a post-Christian world. "We need other maps, other paradigms that might help us change our ways of thinking," noted Pope Francis in his annual Christmas greeting to the Curia in 2019. "We are not in Christianity, not anymore."[23] Or as was captured in the finale to season three of HBO's *Succession*, when Tom asks Greg, "Do you want a deal with the devil?" Greg happily agrees: "What am I gonna do with a soul anyways?" he said. "Souls are boring. Boo, souls."[24]

REMEMBERING THE HOLOCAUST

Many might question whether a culture can really move that quickly from Christian to post-Christian in knowledge and experience, background and familiarity. In truth, the speed by which knowledge can be lost is frightening.

Consider the Holocaust. The first fifty-state survey of Holocaust knowledge among millennials and Generation Z revealed a "worrying lack of basic Holocaust knowledge," including more than one in ten respondents saying they did not recall ever having heard the word *holocaust* before.[25]

The United States Holocaust Memorial Museum's Holocaust Encyclopedia states, "The Holocaust was the systematic, state-sponsored persecution and murder of six million European Jews by the Nazi German regime and its allies and collaborators. The Holocaust was an evolving process that took place throughout Europe between 1933 and 1945. . . . The Nazis believed that the world was divided into distinct races. . . . They considered Germans to be members of the supposedly superior 'Aryan' race. They asserted that 'Aryans' were locked in a struggle for existence with other, inferior races. Further, the Nazis believed that the so-called Jewish race was the most inferior and dangerous of all."[26]

By 1945, using gas vans, killing centers at concentration camps (primarily gas chambers), and firing squads, the Germans and their allies and collaborators killed nearly two out of every three European Jews. *Holocaust* is a word of Greek origin meaning "sacrifice by fire."[27]

Distressing findings from the survey related to this historical event include the following:

- 63 percent of respondents did not know that six million Jewish people were murdered in the Holocaust, and half of those respondents thought the death toll was less than two million.
- Of the forty thousand concentration camps and ghettos established during World War II (such as Auschwitz or Dachau), nearly half of the respondents could not name a single one.
- Only 90 percent of respondents believed the Holocaust happened; 7 percent were not sure and 3 percent denied it occurred.
- 11 percent believed the Jewish people caused the Holocaust.

It doesn't help that about half of those surveyed have seen Holocaust denial or distortion posts online, and 56 percent reported having seen Nazi symbols on social media or in their communities. "The most important lesson is that we can't lose any more time," said Greg Schneider, executive vice president of the Conference on Jewish Material Claims Against Germany (Claims Conference), which commissioned the study. "If we let these trends continue for another generation, the crucial lessons from this terrible part of history could be lost."[28]

This survey's findings and the concerns it raises merit our full attention. But the survey also reminds us how quickly foundational knowledge can be lost, not to mention supplanted by skewed or mistaken understandings.

Including in the Christian faith.

This was one of my central points in my book *Meet Generation Z*, where I wrote, "The most defining characteristic of Generation Z is that it is arguably the first generation in the West (certainly in the United States) that will have been raised in a post-Christian context. As a result, it is the first post-Christian generation. . . . They are not simply living in and being shaped by a post-Christian cultural context. They do not even have a memory of the gospel."[29]

Case in point, according to the "State of the Bible 2022," released by the American Bible Society, nearly 40 percent of Generation Z believe that Jesus was a human and sinned like other people when he lived on earth. There was nothing in their thinking about him that set him apart from any other person.[30] As Gideon Taylor, president of the Claims Conference, noted regarding the Holocaust survey findings, "The results are both shocking and saddening and they underscore why we must act now while Holocaust survivors are still with us to voice their stories. We need to understand why we aren't doing better in educating a younger generation about the Holocaust and the lessons of the past. This needs to serve as a wake-up call to us all."[31]

Yes, it does. And not just about the Holocaust. If it is proving relatively easy for culture at large to forget about the death of six million Jews less than one hundred years ago, imagine how easy it might be to forget about the life of a single Jewish man who died two thousand years earlier.

THE DIGITAL

REVOLUTION

"What the H*** Happened in 2007?"

In 2004 ... Facebook didn't even exist yet, Twitter was still a sound, the cloud was still in the sky, 4G was a parking space, "applications" were what you sent to college ... Big Data was a good name for a rap star, and Skype, for most people, was a typographical error.

—THOMAS FRIEDMAN, *THANK YOU FOR BEING LATE*[1]

There have been many revolutions throughout history.

The French Revolution, beginning in 1789, overthrew the monarchy, established a republic, catalyzed violent periods of political turmoil, and culminated in a dictatorship under Napoleon, who brought many of its principles to areas he conquered in Western Europe and beyond. Historians widely regard the French Revolution as one of the most important events in human history.[2]

Closer to home for many of us is the American Revolution, a colonial revolt that lasted from 1765 to 1783. The American patriots in the thirteen colonies defeated the British with the assistance of France, winning independence from Great Britain and establishing the United States of America. America eventually became a nation of fifty states and is today the world's largest economy by nominal GDP standards, has the largest share of global wealth, is the foremost military power in the world, and is arguably the leading cultural force on the planet.

But neither the French Revolution nor the American Revolution, or any other political revolution, matches the sweeping change brought about by the digital revolution. It may not sound like much, just the development of technology from mechanical and analog to digital, but the digital revolution has changed our world in foundational ways. Not only has it changed how we communicate but it has led us into a new age: the information age.[3] As Eric Schmidt and Jared Cohen have written, there is now a tale of two civilizations: "One is physical and has developed over thousands of years, and the other is virtual and is still very much in formation."[4]

THE DIGITAL REVOLUTION

We call it the digital revolution, but in truth it is the latest in a line of three industrial revolutions. With each, the invention of a technology brought about fundamental societal change. The first industrial revolution started around 1760 in Britain. It was fueled by the invention of the steam engine, which enabled new manufacturing processes, which in turn led to the creation of factories. The second industrial revolution, approximately a century later, was characterized by mass production in new industries such as oil, steel, and electricity. Inventions during this period included the lightbulb, telephone, and internal combustion engine. In the 1960s, the third industrial revolution began with the invention of the semiconductor and led to the inventions of the personal computer and the internet, marking the digital revolution.[5]

But it is only of late that the digital revolution has made its impact most keenly felt, and many missed the moment it descended upon our world like a tsunami. As Pulitzer-Prize-winning *New York Times* columnist Thomas Friedman put it, "What the h*** happened in 2007?" Friedman makes the case that 2007 was one of the most significant pivotal years in all of human history—not simply because that was the year the iPhone was released but because of all that iPhone set in motion and all that came into play in a simultaneous way. Beyond the iPhone, in 2007, Facebook left college campuses and entered the wider world. Twitter was spun off. Google bought YouTube and launched Android. Amazon released the Kindle. And the number of internet users crossed the threshold of one billion worldwide, becoming the fabric of our world.[6] All in 2007. (Friedman neglected to note that also a little company called Netflix began streaming videos in 2007.)

What set off the revolution that year, though, was without a doubt the iPhone. When Steve Jobs introduced the original iPhone as little more than a combination of "three revolutionary projects"—a cellphone, an iPod, and a keyboardless handheld computer with internet connectivity—even he didn't know what had been unleashed. And make no mistake, the iPhone changed the world. It reflects one of the great megashifts of all time: from the physical to the digital. With more than one million apps available by 2013,[7] and nearly

---

IN 2007

- The iPhone was released
- Facebook left college campuses and entered the wider world
- Twitter was spun off
- Google bought YouTube and launched Android
- Netflix began streaming videos
- Amazon released the Kindle
- Internet users surpassed one billion worldwide

two million at the start of 2022,[8] the iPhone has opened the door to what Brian Chen calls the "anything-anytime-anywhere future" where we are constantly connected to a global internet community via hand-held, incredibly capable gadgets with ubiquitous access to data. As Chen aptly titled his book on the matter, we now live in a world that is "always on."[9] I wrote in *Meet Generation Z* that while baby boomers can't remember a world without TV and millennials can't remember a world without computers, "Gen Z does not know a world without constant, immediate and convenient access to the web."[10] And the generation after them? They've already been dubbed Generation Alpha because they will be the first generation "raised in a new world of technological integration."[11] Even e-sports are supplanting the world of physical sports among the youngest of generations. With almost 90 percent of teenagers in the United States in possession of a smartphone, it's not hard to see why.[12]

Of course, it's not simply about smartphones but about smart things.

THE INTERNET OF THINGS

Nearly 70 percent of Americans who have digital assistants use them every day. The number of voice assistants used worldwide will rise from 2.5 billion in 2018 to 8 billion in 2023.[13] In 2018 alone, the number of smart speakers in US households grew by 78 percent (fig. 4.1).[14]

In any given week, we use our smart speakers to play music, get the weather, find answers to questions, set a timer or alarm, or get the news. This is just a taste of the "internet of things" (IoT) that will be unleashed through 5G technology as it sweeps the world. Though 5G might seem like little more than an international upgrade of global phone networks, enabling download speeds at ten to twenty times the previous rate, it's much more. "The evolutionary steps taken to achieve previous generations of wireless technology—2G, 3G and 4G—were akin to traveling from London to Manchester on horseback," says professor

Rahim Tafazolli, founder and director of the 5G Innovation Centre at the University of Surrey. "5G is not an evolutionary step, it is a revolutionary one. We will be jumping off the horse and onto a rocket ship. The sheer speed is only one benefit of the technology. 5G will also allow us to completely transform industries thanks to its ability to connect machines to wireless networks."[15]

FIGURE 4.1
Clutch/Zondervan

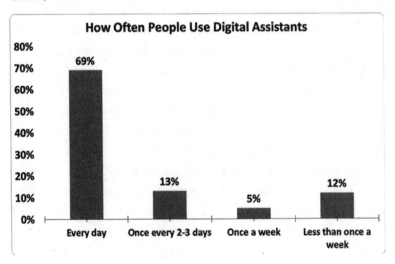

5G will allow IoT devices, "from internet-linked AI speakers to connected cars . . . amounting to a conceptual leap about what the internet is for." Think "autonomous robots in mines, smart cities or super-responsive remote operating theatres—not to mention immersive entertainment that blurs the line between television and video gaming."[16] As an article in *Thred* noted:

> What makes this phenomena so interesting is that these objects could
> theoretically communicate between one another without the need for

human interaction or input. Devices that operate simultaneously and share information are able to send back very specific information to applications or manufacturers, allowing companies to rapidly evolve their products and approaches to tech with increased ease.

The world around us is more responsive as a result of the Internet of Things—and it's only set to become steadily more so.[17]

Currently, even the youngest of generations tends to use the IoT for little more than social media, music, and personal communication. That will change. Generation Z will have grown up in a world of smart objects that will shape not only their thinking but also their experiential expectations. For them, things can and should communicate with each other.

Such technology won't be slowing down. In what is known as Moore's Law, a rule of thumb in the technology industry, processor chips (the small circuit boards that form the backbone of every computing device) double in speed every eighteen months. That means a computer in 2025 will be sixty-four times faster than it was in 2013.[18] Technology has advanced to such a degree that what was once science fiction in films such as *The Matrix* is becoming reality. As the editors of *Wired* noted with the release in 2021 of the fourth installment of the famed movie franchise,

> Your day-to-day reality is an increasingly synthetic experience: Computerized voices inhabit your smart speakers, deepfakes bring dead movie actors back to life, and AI-generated artworks go for eye-watering prices at auction. The simulacrum is extending into food too: Supermarket shelves already contain countless vegan substitutes for meat and other animal products, and before long "real" meat, grown in a lab, will join them. You can inhabit virtual realities and augment your physical one with virtual characters (*Pokemon Go*), street signs (Google Live View), or furniture (Ikea Studio) . . . and

now suddenly everyone is talking about building this thing called "the metaverse."[19]

THE METAVERSE

In 1992, Neal Stephenson released the cyberpunk novel *Snow Crash*. In it, he wrote of an "imaginary place . . . made available to the public over the worldwide fiber-optics network" and then projected onto virtual reality goggles. In it, developers can "build buildings, parks, signs, as well as things that do not exist in Reality, such as vast hovering overhead light shows, special neighborhoods where the rules of three-dimensional spacetime are ignored, and free-combat zones where people can go to hunt and kill each other."

He called it "the Metaverse."[20]

In an attempt to explain in nonfiction terms what the metaverse is, *USA Today* reported that it's "a combination of multiple elements of technology, including virtual reality, augmented reality and video where users 'live' within a digital universe. Supporters of the metaverse envision its users working, playing and staying connected with friends through everything from concerts and conferences to virtual trips around the world."[21]

That vision led Mark Zuckerberg, CEO of Facebook, to change the name of his company to Meta. Zuckerberg described a grandiose vision of the metaverse as an "even more immersive and embodied internet" where "you're gonna be able to do almost anything you can imagine—get together with friends and family, work, learn, play, shop, create—as well as entirely new categories that don't really fit how we think about computers or phones today."[22] If you want a reference point, think of the movie *Avatar*. The metaverse would be a shared social space where avatars represent users, a "world" that avatars interact in and inhabit. In that metaverse, you could own virtual property just as you would physical property or even create your own virtual property, not to mention buy and sell said property. The last step in achieving all of this would be full 3D telepresence via VR or AR glasses. Hubilo Technologies, a technology company that manages hybrid and virtual events, predicts that soon "events will be less about chronology and speakers and more about exploration and interaction. The end of a standard webinar is coming near, being replaced with live-streamed VR entertainment and Oculus Rift parties."[23]

Needless to say, the internet is not going to be "flat" for long.[24] As Matthew Ball, a managing partner at a venture-capital fund investing heavily in the metaverse, writes, "The Metaverse is a massively scaled and interoperable network of real-time rendered 3D virtual worlds which can be experienced synchronously and persistently by an effectively unlimited number of users, and with continuity of data, such as identity, history, entitlements, objects, communications, and payments."[25]

Ian Harber adds that "the metaverse is not *a* digital world. It's a digital world of *worlds* through which people can travel seamlessly, retaining their appearance and digital possessions wherever they go. These worlds do not merely exist in VR (virtual reality), but also layer onto physical reality through AR (augmented reality)."[26]

WEB3

Another dynamic of the digital revolution is the coming of Web 3.0. A typical website during Web 1.0 displayed news and information, or perhaps someone created a personal page reflecting interests or hobbies. Images were discouraged (they took up too much bandwidth), and video was simply not viable. Web 2.0 was more dynamic, more editable, and more user driven. Web pages became interactive and app-like. People signed up for social media accounts and began publishing blogs. Images and video no longer required interminable download times and, as a result, began to be shared in huge numbers.[27]

An article on *Gizmodo* notes that while people define Web3 in different ways, "at its core is the idea of decentralization. . . . Rather than Google, Apple, Microsoft, Amazon and Facebook (sorry, Meta) hoarding everything, the internet will supposedly become more democratized."[28] This is a result of blockchain technology, "which creates publicly visible and verifiable ledgers of record that can be accessed by anyone, anywhere."[29] This is what underpins Bitcoin and other cryptocurrencies, as well as NFTs (nonfungible tokens) which assign permanent ownership to a digital item. Examples include everything from an autographed tweet by the founder of Twitter to digital art.[30] Again, *Gizmodo*: "Web3 is a mix of the two eras that came before it: The advanced, dynamic, app-like tech of the modern web, combined with the decentralized, user-driven philosophy that was around at the start of the internet, before billion- and trillion-dollar corporations owned everything. Web3 shifts the power dynamic from the giant tech entities back to the users. . . . Throw in some artificial intelligence and some machine learning to do everything from filter out unnecessary data to spot security threats, and you've got just about every emerging digital technology covered with Web3."[31]

ARTIFICIAL INTELLIGENCE

Now, about "throwing in" some artificial intelligence (AI). In his book *Life 3.0: Being Human in the Age of Artificial Intelligence*, MIT professor Max Tegmark classifies life forms into three levels of sophistication: Life 1.0, 2.0, and 3.0.[32] Using the terms *hardware* to refer to matter and *software* to refer to information, he deems that Life 1.0 is "life where both the hardware and software are evolved rather than designed." This is simple biological life. Human beings are Life 2.0, "life whose hardware is evolved, but whose software is largely designed." Life 3.0 is life that "can design not only its software but also its hardware. Life 3.0 is the master of its own destiny, finally free from its evolutionary shackles."[33] So if bacteria are Life 1.0 and humans are Life 2.0, what is Life 3.0?

Artificial intelligence.

Or to be specific, artificial general intelligence (AGI). Rudimentary forms of AI are already with us in everything from the facial recognition software in Apple's iPhone to our digital assistants Siri, Alexa, and Cortana. The holy grail for tech developers is AGI, which is AI reaching human-level intelligence and beyond, able to accomplish virtually any goal, including learning. So Life 1.0 is biological, Life 2.0 is cultural, and Life 3.0 is technological.

Multiple questions surround AI, not the least of which are theological questions, such as, "How do we understand AGI in light of the view that humankind is made in God's image? How does AGI change our definition of life?" There is also the goal of AI to reflect upon. Almost all who work on AI agree that the goal should be to develop not undirected intelligence but beneficial intelligence. The main concern isn't with robots but with intelligence itself—intelligence whose goals are destructive. As Tegmark notes, "We might build technology powerful enough to permanently end [social] scourges—or to end humanity itself. We might create societies that flourish like never before, on Earth and perhaps beyond, or a Kafkaesque global surveillance state so powerful that it could never be toppled."[34]

Of all that is happening in and through the digital revolution, AI is the most controversial. Tesla and SpaceX CEO Elon Musk told a National Governors Association meeting that his exposure to AI technology suggests it poses "a fundamental risk to the existence of human civilization." Just before his death, cosmologist Stephen Hawking agreed, saying that AI could prove "the worst event in the history of civilization." Meta founder Mark Zuckerberg, however, calls such talk "irresponsible."[35]

No wonder the conversation about AI has been called the most important of our time. As an article in *Christianity Today* notes, "[AI] raises a number of challenging moral and spiritual questions. Facial recognition can be used to locate fugitive criminals, but also to suppress political dissidents. Various apps and platforms can anticipate our preferences, but also harvest data that invades our privacy. Technology can speed healing, but many are hoping to use it to enhance natural human abilities or eliminate 'undesirable' emotions."[36]

One of the leading Christian thinkers on all things AI is Oxford professor John Lennox, who understands the many benefits AI has to offer but is also keenly aware of the worldview that lies behind many of the secular visions that "seek to transform humans into gods and create utopias through technology."[37] Lennox concludes, "But every technological invention has potentiality for good and evil. The issue is not that one resists advance, but one learns to control that advance and set it into an ethical framework."[38]

OVERWHELMED YET?

If you a feel bit behind the curve on all things digital, you're not alone. According to a Pew Research Center survey, a majority of US adults can answer fewer than half the questions correctly on a digital knowledge quiz, and many struggle with cybersecurity and privacy questions (fig. 4.2).[39]

Craig Mundie, a supercomputer designer and former chief of strategy and research at Microsoft, notes that when the rate of change begins to exceed the ability to adapt, dislocation is inevitable. Dislocation is different from disruption. Disruption occurs when someone does something clever that makes you or your company look obsolete. Dislocation is when the whole environment is being altered at such speed that everyone starts to feel like they can't keep up. "The world is not just rapidly changing," adds Dov Seidman, "it is being dramatically reshaped—it is starting to operate differently."[40]

Yet the speed of technological change does not allow for much of a learning curve. Think about the telephone. It took seventy-five years for one hundred million people to gain access to the telephone; in 2016 the gaming app Pokemon Go was able to hook that many people on playing it in less than a single month.[41]

FIGURE 4.2
Pew Research Center

Many Americans are unsure about a number of digital topics

% of U.S. adults answering each question ...

	Incorrectly	Correctly	Not sure
Phishing scams can occur on social media, websites, email or text messages	18	67	15
Cookies allow websites to track user visits and site activity	9	63	27
Advertising is largest source of revenue for most social media platforms	9	59	32
Privacy policies are contracts between websites and users about how those sites will use their data	25	48	27
Net neutrality describes principle that internet service providers should treat all traffic on their networks equally	12	45	42
"https://" in a URL means that information entered into the site is encrypted	15	30	53
WhatsApp and Instagram are both owned by Facebook	22	29	49
Can identify example of true two-factor authentication (set of images)	55	28	17
Private browsing mode only prevents someone using the same computer from seeing one's online activities	25	24	49
Can correctly identify picture of Jack Dorsey	7	15	77

Note: Those who did not give an answer are not shown. All questions are multiple choice; for full question wording, see topline.
Source: Survey conducted June 3-17, 2019.
"Americans and Digital Knowledge"

PEW RESEARCH CENTER

There can be little doubt that we live in a technological age and have embraced technological advance with abandon, creating what Neil Postman termed a "technopoly," where technology of every kind is cheerfully granted sovereignty.[42] Yet as Postman notes, technology "is both friend and enemy."[43] Since I will argue in much of this book for the importance of embracing technology as friend for the sake of the church's mission, it is important to begin with a word about technology as a potential enemy to accurately conveying the message of the gospel.

The Medium Is
the Massage

*Supposing there had been a fourth temptation
when our Lord encountered the devil in the
wilderness—this time an offer of networked
TV appearances, in prime time, to proclaim
and expound his gospel. Would this offer,
too, have been rejected like the others?*
—MALCOLM MUGGERIDGE, *CHRIST AND THE MEDIA* [1]

Marshall McLuhan, a Canadian philosopher whose work is essential in the study of media theory, is famous for arguing that "the medium is the message." [2] His point was that the way we gain information affects us more than the information itself does. In a book whose title is a twist on his own phrase, *The Medium Is the Massage*, McLuhan explains his central thesis: "All media work us over completely. They are so pervasive in their personal, political, economic, aesthetic, psychological, moral, ethical, and social consequences that they leave no part of us untouched, unaffected, unaltered. The medium is the massage. Any understanding of social and cultural change is impossible without a knowledge of the way media work as environments."[3]

His point is the medium is *socially* the message/massage because "it is the medium that shapes and controls the scale and form of human association and action."[4] Specifically, when McLuhan refers to a medium *conveying*, he does not mean facts or knowledge but of "the response of our physical senses to the medium." He wants to expand our thinking of a medium as more than just a conveyor of content and to see the medium itself as having influence. "The content of a movie is a novel or a play or an opera," he wrote in his seminal work *Understanding Media*. "The effect of the movie form is not related to its program content."[5]

In this regard, he speaks of hot and cool mediums. A hot medium offers something well-defined and detailed—think radio, print, photographs, and movies. Such mediums give a great deal of information and don't require the user to fill in the blanks. They are simply read or watched. A cool medium offers images and forms and shapes that are less distinct and provide little information, forcing the user to work harder and fill in what is missing. Think telephone, cartoons, and television. For example, television, being less immersive than a movie viewed in a theater, requires more from the person engaging it as a medium. It should be noted that McLuhan, who died in 1981, did not have the digital revolution as we understand it today, much less the internet, in his thinking as much as the world of television and film (though he did predict something along the lines of what we now call the internet). The internet does not fall neatly into a hot or cold category. It is hot in the sense of detail and amount of information while being cool in the sense of being highly participatory and interactive. Since the discussion is about how a medium engages our senses, it could be argued that the internet, not to mention virtual reality (VR), is the most engaging of all mediums.[6]

Neil Postman gives a more pointed critique, lamenting "the decline of the Age of Typography and the ascendancy of the Age of Television."[7] Postman's central contention, that "the media of communication available to a culture are a dominant influence on the formation of the culture's intellectual and social preoccupations," is without question.[8] Yet there is an overly dismissive nature within Postman's critique, most evident in the insignificance he gives to the ministry of the famed evangelist Billy Graham—that because Graham's ministry was television based, he is only an "image, a picture of a face. . . . Of words, almost nothing comes to mind."[9] This, of course, is simply not true. We may think of a face, but there were most certainly words attached to Graham's image that changed countless lives despite the medium.

But that we live in a media-dominated culture is irrefutable. Todd Gitlin, who chaired the PhD program in communications at Columbia University, suggested that "the torrent of images, songs, and stories streaming has become our familiar world."[10] Playing off of McLuhan's famous phrase, Gitlin suggested that the "montage is the message."[11] Gitlin called this new supersaturation of the media the "media torrent," which determines what we see and what we don't, what we think about, and what never enters our minds.

Gitlin offered a parable about a customs officer who observes a truck pulling up at the border. Suspicious, the officer conducts a painstaking search of the vehicle but finds nothing. This begins a pattern where, week after week, the driver approaches the border, the truck is searched, but nothing is found. Yet the customs officer is convinced that there is contraband. Finally, after many years, the officer is set to retire. Once again, the driver pulls up, and the officer says, "I know you're a smuggler. . . . Don't bother denying it. But . . . [I can't] figure out what you've been smuggling all these years. I'm leaving now. I swear to you I can do you no harm. Won't you please tell me what you've been smuggling?"

"Trucks," the driver says.

Gitlin's point? The media have been smuggling the habit of living with the media.[12]

THE SHALLOWS

In his book *The Shallows: What the Internet Is Doing to Our Brains*, Nicholas Carr agrees with McLuhan "that in the long run a medium's content matters less than the medium itself in influencing how we think and act. . . . A popular medium molds what we see and how we see it—and eventually, if we use it enough, it changes who we are, as individuals and as a society."[13]

The medium is not related only to the message but there is also a strong relationship between the medium and the person using the medium. Carr goes on to outline how the very nature of the internet is making us shallow thinkers. Our brains change in response to experiences—they are plastic, if you will—which means the various technologies we use to search, gather, and convey information can actually reroute our neural pathways.

Of particular concern are what Carr calls "information technologies," which include "all the tools we use to extend or support our mental powers—to find and classify information, to formulate and articulate ideas, to share know-how and knowledge, to take measurements and perform calculations, to expand the capacity of our memory."[14]

Here is the heart of Carr's concern and the essence of his book:

Dozens of studies by psychologists, neurobiologists, educators, and web designers point to the same conclusion: when we go online, we enter an environment that promotes cursory reading, hurried and distracted thinking, and superficial learning. . . .

One thing is very clear: if, knowing what we know today about the brain's plasticity, you were to set out to invent a medium that would rewire our mental circuits as quickly and thoroughly as possible, you would probably end up designing something that looks and works a lot like the internet.[15]

WHAT THE ONLINE WORLD IS DOING TO US

Generation Z spends, on average, nine hours a day in front of one screen or another—TV, video games, smartphones, or tablets.[16] What does that level of online consumption do to individuals and society in general? We know that it is having a negative effect in at least five areas.

First, it's hurting our kids. According to a major study of nearly ten thousand teenagers by University College London and Imperial College London, social media damages children's mental health by "ruining sleep, reducing their exercise levels and exposing them to cyberbullies in their homes." In fact, "using sites multiple times a day increases the risk of psychological distress by around 40 percent, compared to logging on weekly or less."[17]

Making matters worse, children's screen time doubled during the pandemic and, according to researchers from the University of California—San Francisco, hasn't gone down since. Adding to the concern is that screen time does not include time spent on computers for schoolwork; researchers focused exclusively on recreational activities such as social media, texting, internet surfing, and watching or streaming movies.[18]

Second, it's changing how we view and have sex. A survey from the UK's *Times* finds that pornography is leading to sex where women getting hurt is the new normal, specifically the causing of pain and humiliation. BDSM (bondage and discipline, dominance and submission, sadism, and masochism) "is now ordinary." Slapping, choking, anal intercourse—internet pornography has made those who view these things expect them.[19] For Generation Z, "rough sex" (hair pulling, biting, slapping, choking, and other aggressive behavior) is now the second most popular porn category searched, and nearly half say online porn is the source of their sex education. It's also changing our experience with sex, creating distance with our sexual partners, both emotionally and physically. Those who watch porn often find themselves unable to be sexually aroused by their actual flesh-and-blood partners.[20]

Billie Eilish, one of the biggest Gen Z musical stars and the youngest person in history to win all four of the top Grammy awards in the same year, has spoken freely about her addiction to pornography, which started at age eleven. It not only gave her nightmares but affected her later dating life. Speaking on the *Howard Stern Show* on Sirius XM radio, she said, "I think it really destroyed my brain and I feel incredibly devastated that I was exposed to so much porn." Twenty years old at the time of the interview, she added, "The first few times I, you know, had sex, I was not saying no to things that were not good. It was because I thought that's what I was supposed to be attracted to."[21]

Third, it's costing us community, or at least previously available dynamics of community. Consider dating. Singles today complain about the pitfalls and disappointments of online dating, as if it is the only kind of dating there is. In truth, online dating represents a radical cultural departure from what used to be the norm. It is radically individualistic, as opposed to the more communally based dating of the recent past. Instead of friends and family making suggestions and introductions, it is now an algorithm and two rightward swipes. As an article in the *Atlantic* puts it, "Robots are not yet replacing our jobs. But they're supplanting the role of matchmaker once held by friends and family.... [For] centuries, most couples met the same way: They relied on their families and friends to set them up. In sociology-speak, our relationships were 'mediated.' In human-speak, your wingman was your dad."[22]

> ## WHAT THE ONLINE WORLD IS DOING TO US
>
> 1. It's hurting our kids.
> 2. It's changing how we view and have sex.
> 3. It's costing us community.
> 4. It's making us angrier.
> 5. It's fueling rapid cultural change.

Tinder, OKCupid, and Bumble have taken the place of community. No longer are those most intimate with us serving and guiding and counseling; "now . . . we're getting by with a little help from our robots." Even those most involved in online dating lament "the spiritual bankruptcy of modern love." Or as one person put it, the rise of online dating reflects "heightened isolation and a diminished sense of belonging within communities."[23]

Fourth, it's making us angrier. Polling reveals two things we all seem to agree on: people are more likely to express anger on social media than in person (nearly nine in ten), and we are angrier today compared with a generation ago (84 percent). According to an NPR–IBM Watson Health Poll, the more we go online to check the news or use social media, the angrier we become. The reasons are not hard to diagnose: news outlets are often openly biased toward a particular view (thus inciting emotions), and there is rampant trolling on social media. We've created a context for anger to be incited and expressed, and it's working.[24] News outlets have found that the more they can tap into fears or anger, the higher the ratings.[25]

Finally, living online is fueling the rapid change of culture, and not always for the best. For example, there are few changes that have swept the cultural landscape more swiftly than the West flipping its views on homosexuality. As recently as 2004, polls conducted by the Pew Research Center showed that the majority of Americans (60 percent) opposed same-sex marriage. Today, 61 percent support it. How did minds change so quickly? In a telling study, Harvard University psychology professor Mahzarin Banaji investigated long-term changes in attitudes. She found that between 2007 and 2016, bias toward people who are gay decreased dramatically.[26] Many dynamics could be associated with this shift, such as the growing visibility of gay people in popular culture (such as Ellen DeGeneres, the show *Will and Grace*), but why did the landslide toward cultural acceptance begin in 2007? As we saw earlier, that was the year the iPhone was released, Facebook left college campuses, Twitter was spun off, Google bought YouTube and launched Android, Amazon released the Kindle, and the number of internet users crossed the threshold of one billion worldwide. There can be little doubt that social media accelerates cultural change—for good or ill.

IS IT TIME TO BECOME A LUDDITE?

In the nineteenth century, a group of English textile workers known as Luddites (the origin of the name is unclear) protested against manufacturers and their increasing use of textile machinery. Radical factions of these workers even took it upon themselves to destroy the machinery. They were threatened by the changes the machines were bringing, most notably the marginalization of their craft as the machines replaced the need for their skills. Adding to their angst was that many of the Luddites were owners of small workshops that went out of business because large-scale factories could sell the same products for less money. Factories had few job openings for these displaced workers because they needed fewer employees than the workshops did to make the same product. Unemployed and angry, the Luddites revolted against all things mechanical. The rebellion, lasting from 1811 to 1816, was eventually suppressed with legal and military force. Today the term *Luddite* has become a name for someone who is "opposed to industrialization, automation, computerization, or new technologies in general."[27]

So does the dark side of the digital world call for becoming a Luddite? Jaron Lanier made waves with his little book *Ten Arguments for Deleting Your Social Media Accounts Right Now*, even if for just a short detox. He recounts some of these arguments in his final chapter: "To review: Your understanding of others has been disrupted because you don't know what they've experienced in their feeds, while the reverse is also true; the empathy others might offer you is challenged because you can't know the context in which you'll be understood. You're probably becoming more of an a**hole, but you're also probably sadder. . . . Your ability to know the world, to know truth, has been degraded, while the world's ability to know you has been corrupted. Politics has become unreal and terrifying, while economics has become unreal and unsustainable."[28]

So where does this leave a Christ follower?

The answer is in an unavoidable tension.

Unavoidable Tension

I see that Christ is needed in television studios.
—MOTHER TERESA¹

The digital revolution, and the cultural concerns that go with it, undoubtedly presents the church with a profound tension. On the one hand, digital technology promises the gospel and the church greater reach than at any other time in human history. On the other hand, there are understandable reasons, and in some cases serious concerns, to hesitate to use it. Is there a medium that is so much a message that using it distorts the gospel beyond recognition? Does a medium like television reduce any and all content to a mere image absent of any true content? Should the church engage or resist the media torrent? Does the dark side of being online warrant a Luddite mindset in the church?

These questions should keep us from thoughtlessly embracing technology. As Felicia Wu Song writes in *Restless Devices*, "We have clearly moved into a new cultural moment where many of us feel a twinge of regret about the impoverishing effects of our digital engagement on our lives."² She's not alone in feeling this way. According to the *Washington*

Post, "Only 10 percent say Facebook has a positive impact on society, while 56 percent say it has a negative impact and 33 percent say its impact is neither positive nor negative. Even among those who use Facebook daily, more than three times as many say the social network has a negative rather than a positive impact." Yet in the same *Washington Post* article, full-time mom Mary Veselka says, "We go into it knowing that we can't really trust them, but I don't think we can get around not using it."[3]

The church must not only live with this tension but also embrace it. The digital revolution has already taken place and has changed the way the world communicates and relates. To refuse to thoughtfully and prayerfully engage our digital world despite its dark side would be theologically misguided and missiologically ruinous. In *The Shallows*, Nicholas Carr wondered whether "Google may yet turn out to be a flash in the pan."[4] No one has that kind of naivete today.

But what of those who would contend that the church must not embrace digital forms of communication because, as Marshall McLuhan argued, the medium is the message, and the mediums we use might run counter to what we hope to achieve? As Song writes, by using some mediums, the church "runs the risk of either naively promoting or remaining dangerously silent about digital habits that are slowly but surely distorting the very understanding and experience of soul formation and genuine Christian discipleship."[5]

Such sentiments are frequently voiced, but they often come across as just sentiments—attitudes or opinions based on personal preference. As I've often told my graduate students, we must be very careful not to build theological fences around personal tastes. And I sense there are many who simply do not like it when a church embraces the digital world. They don't want to read a book on Kindle, they don't want to attend a class online, they don't want to gather in virtual community, they don't like the feel of an online campus, and from such sentiments, they go into Adam Grant's preacher or prosecutor mode, as we saw in the introduction.

Evidence of how this sentiment can play out can be found in varying perspectives even within the same publication. For example, Bonnie Kristian opined in *Christianity Today*, "The medium will meaningfully reframe or outright change the message—chiefly, I suspect, by trivializing it and pulling our attention away."[6] But Kyuboem Lee, also writing in *Christianity Today*, sees things differently. He notes that we have become "overly dependent on a mode of church that invests most of our time, efforts, and financial resources on large-gathering productions on Sundays."[7]

Returning to those who would disqualify many mediums because "the medium is the message": while McLuhan has some telling points, he was not trying to make the difference between medium and message something nefarious. His point was that a book and the movie adaptation of that book are two different mediums that can affect us in two different ways. It doesn't mean the story is always altered beyond recognition. Sometimes, the movie adaptation can make the story more penetrating and accessible than before.

But even if there is validity to some Christians' concerns, the reality of our moment is that digital mediums are a primary way our world communicates and relates. And we must use the digital tools at our disposal even if for no other reason than to call people away from the digital and into the physical so they can experience the full measure of spiritual formation and communal life. There can be little doubt that, as Jay Y. Kim has written, in a digital age we will still need an "analog church"— real people, real places, and real things.[8] The digital revolution does not mean we have stopped being humans with real needs. But the reality is that the only way to continue the human interaction and transformation the church uniquely provides is to bridge the digital divide. It will take the digital to both maintain and, in areas where it is desperately needed, call people to the physical.

I am contending for thoughtful engagement of digital tools for the sake of the evangelistic cause. Moving forward, most of the church's initial contact with a lost world will be digital. We must use digital mediums to connect with our world in order to call people back to God. As Gitlin concludes, whether we like it or not, "We must imagine the whole phenomenon freshly, taking the media seriously . . . as a central condition of an entire way of life."[9] There is a difference between being a thoughtless adopter and a cultural missionary. And make no mistake, our mission field has changed dramatically.

Digital engagement can be done thoughtfully and biblically. As Tim Challies has argued, if one response is an enthusiastic and uncritical embrace, and a second calls for strict separation, then consider a third way: "disciplined discernment."[10] Alan Noble suggests four questions we should ask before using any medium:[11]

1. What kinds of messages is this medium typically used to convey?
2. What connotations, images, and connections will people make with this message in this medium?
3. Am I communicating the truth of my message in this form?
4. Will others perceive the radical uniqueness of this message, or will they categorize it as yet another consumer choice?

We can disagree about what the answers might be, but asking such questions should be a given.

Let's do away with the glib remarks that you can't do church digitally. The goal is not to transform the church into a solely digital form but to transform the church's thinking and methods and strategies in order to reach a post-Christian world. Accomplishing this goal will necessarily include taking full advantage of the digital revolution. We must embrace a hybrid model of ministry that involves the digital and the physical because that is the reality of our world. Though we might be more comfortable with physical approaches we are familiar with, let's also have a healthy sense of humility about evaluating what the digital world offers. What is often overlooked is how a particular new medium might enhance instead of diminish. Different is not always worse. The truth for many churches is that we've done things a certain way for so long that we may not realize that the very definitions of *places* and *things*—even what it means to be in human community—have changed.

Theologian Millard Erickson, building on the insights of William E. Hordern, notes that every generation must translate the gospel into its unique cultural context. But this is very different from *transforming* the message of the gospel into something that was never intended by the biblical witness. Transformation of the message must be avoided at all costs. Translation, however, is essential for a winsome and compelling presentation of the gospel of Christ.[12] And every leader must navigate this interplay. If transformation takes place, then we have abandoned orthodoxy for the sake of obtaining more warm bodies; the tickling of ears is not exactly welcomed in the Bible. But if translation takes place, we build bridges of cultural understanding while retaining our prophetic voice in the marketplace of ideas.

Transformation is heresy.

Translation is the heart of our mission.[13]

SALT, LIGHT, AND THE THIRD WAY

The early Christian church had a nickname that many Christians are unaware of. It was known as the Third Way. This title appeared as early as the second century.[14] It was a reference to how some religious expressions catered to culture by co-opting and reflecting it, while others isolated themselves from it. As Gerald Sittser has written, the first would have "undermined the uniqueness of their belief system and way of life," and the second "would have kept them safe on the margins—safe, . . . but irrelevant."[15]

Instead, Christians did neither. They chose a third way that engaged the world while not compromising their beliefs. As is commonly put, they were in the world, but not of it. There is nothing needed more in our post-Christian, digital world than men and women committed to the third way—people who have the unfiltered gospel in one hand and the internet in the other, with a heart beating for the lost.

So rather than decry a church's foray into technology or the online world or the metaverse, consider anew Jesus' words: "You are the salt of the earth. But if the salt loses its saltiness, how can it be made salty again? It is no longer good for anything, except to be thrown out and trampled underfoot. You are the light of the world. A town on a hill cannot be hidden. Neither do people light a lamp and put it under a bowl. Instead they put it on its stand, and it gives light to everyone in the house. In the same way, let your light shine before others, that they may see your good deeds and glorify your Father in heaven" (Matt. 5:13–16).

In Jesus' day, salt was one of the most useful and important elements, but it wasn't because of what it did for the taste of food. Back then, salt was mainly used as a preservative. People didn't have refrigerators or freezers, and they couldn't buy things in cans, so they used salt to keep their food from spoiling. If you had a piece of meat that you couldn't eat right away, you'd rub some salt into it and that would keep the meat from decaying. When Jesus said we should be like salt, he meant that we should live in such a way that our very presence in the world staves off decay. John Stott once wrote that "the world is . . . putrefying. It cannot stop itself from going bad. Only salt introduced from outside can do this. The church . . . is set in the world . . . as salt to arrest—or at least to hinder—the process of social decay. . . . God intends the most powerful of all restraints within sinful society to be his own redeemed, regenerate and righteous people."[16]

Jesus also called us to make a difference by being the light of the world. Whereas salt is about taking a stand, light is about revealing what is real; it's about showing the way. To let our lights shine is to make known what Christ is doing in our lives and the truth about what Christ wants to do in everyone's lives. So you can think of it this way: Salt is a negative influence: it works *against* something. Light is a positive influence: it tries to *bring* something. Both are needed for influence. We work against moral and cultural decay; we work for truth. Again, Stott: "One can hardly blame unsalted meat for going bad. It cannot do anything else. The real question to ask is, 'Where is the salt?'"[17]

The online world is unsalted meat.

And if we fail in our mission to be the salt of the earth? What if the salt loses its saltiness? Jesus makes it clear: if salt doesn't function like salt, it is worthless. Some people seem to think that Christians' goal is to retain as much salt for themselves and in themselves as possible. They think the way to keep salt from losing its saltiness is to retreat from the world, to make sure they don't interact with it so they don't get polluted and lose any of their saltiness. But that is the opposite of what Jesus is saying. According to him, the way to lose our saltiness, the way to become irrelevant, to have no influence at all, to make the salt in our lives meaningless, is to keep from interacting with the decay of the world.

Avoiding interaction with the world will ensure not only that the world dies but that your church will too. This is the way salt works: it is either used proactively or it becomes destructive to the one who has it. Think of the Dead Sea. Why is it dead, with no life in it at all? It is because it has such heavy mineral content that the water cannot support life of any kind. There's no outlet for the water that flows in. If water doesn't flow out, it stagnates. It can't support life. It dies.

Or think of our bodies. If they don't give off salt through perspiration, we retain water and become bloated, and eventually, we can develop all kinds of medical complications leading to death. What's true in nature and true of our bodies is true for the church. The goal is not to keep ourselves as salty as possible by retreating from the world but to keep ourselves as salty as possible so that we can give that salt to the world, and we should do so where it is decaying the most. In this case, instead of the medium being the message, the message can shape the medium.

65

Malcolm Muggeridge tells of taking Mother Teresa into a New York television studio to appear on one of the morning shows. It was the first time Mother Teresa had been in an American television studio, and she was completely unprepared for the constant interruptions for commercials. On that particular morning, all of the commercials dealt with food that was being advertised as "nonfattening and non-nourishing."[18] Mother Teresa, noted Muggeridge, looked at them with a kind of wonder, "her own constant preoccupation being, of course, to find the wherewithal to nourish the starving and put some flesh on human skeletons. It took some little time for the irony of the situation to strike her. When it did, she remarked, in a perfectly audible voice: 'I see that Christ is needed in television studios.'"[19]

Yes, he is.

TECHNOLOGY BEHIND A REFORMATION

The impetus behind Martin Luther's posting his Ninety-Five Theses on All Saint's Eve, October 31, 1517, was the church's sale of indulgences. An indulgence was a pardon granted by the church so that a person could avoid punishment for their sins. In essence, indulgences borrowed from the storehouse of merit earned by Jesus and the saints. The idea was that the head of the church was in charge of this storehouse. In Luther's time, the granting of indulgences was "vulgarized and commercialized by mountebanks and professional pardon-peddlers."[20]

Like Johann Tetzel.

Tetzel worked Luther's part of the world, and his sale of indulgences pushed Luther over the edge. All people had to do was pay a certain sum and they would receive a promise of full escape from punishment in purgatory. No confession needed. You could even arrange to buy such an indulgence for a friend who was already there. Tetzel's pitch: "When a coin in the coffer rings, / a soul from purgatory springs."[21]

Posting a response on the door of a church, a glorified bulletin board, seems mild by most standards. It was also relatively common for the day, a regular feature of university life and the typical way of giving notice for debate. And the University of Wittenberg itself was a somewhat obscure institution in a rather small town of dirty streets and mud houses with straw roofs. So when Luther posted his Ninety-Five Theses, there was no expectation that it would prompt anything more than a bit of local debate. Instead, a revolution was born that led to the Protestant Reformation and the upending of the political and ecclesiastical order throughout Europe.

Why did a handwritten document posted on a church door in Wittenberg become so influential? The better question is how, and the answer is technology. A few decades earlier, a new invention—the printing press—had come into play, and German printers sensed that Luther's broadside might sell. "As an entrepreneurial venture, they set the *Ninety-Five Theses* into type, printed them and reproduced them," notes Tom Rassieur, who curated the largest gathering of objects related to Luther for the Minneapolis Institute of Art. "When they saw how rapidly they were selling, they made copies and copies and copies. It went viral." Rassieur's exhibition included several versions of the printed theses, including a pocket-sized edition. One copy was printed in Basel (present-day Switzerland) not more than two months after Luther posted his handwritten version. "That means Luther's words had already reached out hundreds of miles," Rassieur says. "When Luther's ideas started to spread, there was no way they could be stopped." While no one knows how many copies were eventually printed, Rassieur estimates there were "thousands and thousands." Tom Gjelten reported on the exhibit for NPR: "As with the internet centuries later, Luther showed how a new information technology could change the world."[22]

Perhaps it's time for another reformation. When asked whether God was in cyberspace, Thomas Friedman quipped, "No, but he wants to be there."[23]

INTERLUDE

Church 3.0

If we are to better the future, we
must disturb the present.
—CATHERINE BOOTH[1]

It is time to put forward a simple but provocative thesis: the church must respond to the new reality of a post-Christian world and the digital revolution by becoming something it has never been before. Church 3.0.

The church must respond this way, first, because the rise of the nones and the post-Christian world we live in have changed our mission field entirely and, second, because the digital revolution has changed our means of communicating with that mission field. The significance of these changes cannot be overstated. When you look at the cultural challenge facing the mission of the church, regardless of the era, two key dynamics have always been at play: one is the nature of the mission field, and the second is the nature of communication needed to reach that mission field.

Imagine you are sent to reach an unreached people group, such as the Shaikh of Bangladesh. You first need to know something about the spiritual state of those people. What religious or supernatural beliefs do they hold? Have they been exposed in any way to the Christian faith? Understanding your mission field is understanding who you are trying to reach—economically, culturally, demographically, and especially spiritually. In this case, you find yourself in South Asia on the Bay of Bengal. The dominant religion of the Shaikh is Islam—they practice both Sunni and Shia traditions—and there are many subgroups within the Shaikh people group. Just that small snapshot tells you many things you need to know and do to prepare as a missionary. Next, you need to learn how to communicate with them. You need to learn their language—in this case, Bengali—and then convey the message of the Christian faith in a way that is both understandable and accessible.

Now let's imagine you want to reach an entire culture, not just a particular people group. What can be said of the West as a mission field, and how have we historically communicated with Western culture? For example, is the climate Christian, anti-Christian, post-Christian? What is the spiritual context in which we are trying to operate? Is the culture literate and knowledgeable? If not, what is the nature of its illiteracy and ignorance? Then we must ask how people communicate with each other within that culture, which is key because that will determine how we must communicate the gospel. Have our theology and Scriptures even been translated into that language yet?

FIRST CHURCH ERA

PENTECOST TO AD 310

Spiritual Climate: Pagan
Communication: Oral
Response: Church 1.0

As I've said, there have been only three main eras in the roughly two-thousand-year history of the church. The first era began with the birth of the church. Following Pentecost, the early church faced a largely pagan culture that used premodern modes of communication. What kind of church evolved to meet this challenge? Let's call it Church 1.0.

Church 1.0 was organic and communal. It met in homes and often faced persecution. Leadership was strong, authority was established, but structure was loose knit. Communication was almost entirely oral. Even when a letter from, say, the apostle Paul arrived, the custom was to read it aloud to the gathered church.

Evangelism was designed largely for Jews, Judaizing gentiles, and pagans. Churches networked with each other but largely focused on, and reflected, their immediate context. This is why the New Testament letters vary in content. The context at Corinth, for example, was vastly different from the context at Rome. But in all the churches, signs and wonders flowed relatively freely, particularly early on, authenticating the early proclamation of the gospel. When signs and wonders were combined with an emphasis on personal evangelism and service to the poor and vulnerable, the numbers of converts exploded. By AD 100, there were around 7,500 followers worldwide. By the mid-300s, more than thirty million called themselves followers of Christ.[2]

Then everything changed.

The growth and influence of the Christian movement, particularly after the conversion of Roman Emperor Constantine in 310, transformed the West from a pagan culture to a Christian culture. But that wasn't the only thing that changed. So did communication, which evolved from oral to written, and then to mechanized writing. How did the church respond? What kind of church emerged to meet the challenge of not only a changed spiritual context but also new forms of communication—to meet the challenge of going from persecuted minority to dominant cultural majority, and from an oral mode of communication to a written mode? Let's call it Church 2.0.

> **SECOND CHURCH ERA**
>
> *AD 310 TO POST-ENLIGHTENMENT*
>
> Spiritual Climate: Christian
> Communication: Written and Mechanized
> Response: Church 2.0

71

As we saw in chapter 1, Church 2.0 spanned a long section of Christian history, from the early Middle Ages to the time known as the Enlightenment and to the modern era. While much changed in the West during that time, one thing did not: the centrality of the church and the Christian faith. What this meant was that rather than contending for Christ in a marketplace of ideas, as well as in the face of persecution, the Western church operated in a context of cultural dominance, if not outright control.

As for communication, the Scriptures were canonized and their propagation was confined to written language—Hebrew, Greek, Latin, and eventually German, English, and other languages. This meant that communication shifted from primarily oral to primarily written, and then it became mechanized. It should be no surprise that the very first book off Gutenberg's revolutionary movable-type printing press in 1454 was a Bible.

We are now living in the aftermath of a seismic change as Western culture completed its shift from Christian to post-Christian. The church and the Christian faith had a tight grip on culture for more than a thousand years, and the shift from sacred to secular, from Christian to post-Christian, took from the Enlightenment era until now to take place. And communication has shifted from mechanized writing to electronic encoding. We are now living in a post-Christian digital world.

THIRD CHURCH ERA

2010S TO THE PRESENT

Spiritual Climate: Post-Christian
Communication: Digital
Response: Church 3.0

What kind of church will meet the challenge of this new day? Let's call it Church 3.0.

Church 3.0 embraces the new post-Christian digital terrain. Knowing that you're trying to reach a post-Christian world, not pre-Christian or Christian, and knowing that you have to do it digitally is a paradigm shift of seismic proportions. And change has happened so fast that we're having to, as they say, fly the plane while we build it. This third missional era has come into being in a historical nanosecond. We live in a profoundly different context than we did even twenty years ago, which is why it is so important for the church to wake up immediately to a new set of realities. Do you know the analogy of the frog in the kettle? If you place a frog in a pot of water and slowly warm the temperature of the water to a boiling point, the frog won't notice that the water has become too hot until it's too late. The frog will be dead before it knows to jump out. This illustration was often used to waken churches to the slowly warming waters of cultural change.[3] But our situation is more akin to a frog in a microwave. We're not easing into this. It's not a gradual change. It's abrupt, which means we have to adapt quickly. We simply can't do church in a 1.0 or 2.0 way anymore.

Becoming Church 3.0 means going hybrid. We must be a community of faith *and* a church for the unchurched. We must have a physical *and* a digital presence.

In the chapters that follow, we will explore four ways that churches can rise to the cultural moment: take advantage of the internet, embrace the new community, become a church for the unchurched, and think strategically.

"IT'S THE INTERNET, STUPID"

Opening the Digital Front Door

The digital genie is out of the bottle. Your church is still around. The church is still around. It's just leaving the building.

—CAREY NIEUWHOF[1]

James Carville was the lead political strategist for the successful election of Bill Clinton, then governor of Arkansas, to the presidency of the United States. He distilled the campaign to three messages: "Change versus more of the same," "Don't forget health care," and most important, "It's the economy, stupid." The US was in the midst of an economic recession, and Clinton's incessant focus on the economy unseated President George H. W. Bush, despite Bush's receiving a 90 percent approval rating following the invasion of Kuwait. But Carville was right in seeing that the real issue, what mattered most to people, was the economy, and then painting Clinton as the one best able to turn it around.

If I had to distill a message to pastors, church leaders, and anyone interested in the vitality of the church, it would be this: "It's the internet, stupid." Why? It's where the majority of the people you are trying to reach and serve live. Americans, on average, visit more than eight websites a day, amounting to more than three thousand websites per year. As Kinjil Mathur, chief marketing officer at Squarespace, said, "Browsing the web plays a central role in our daily lives."[2] One could even argue that it plays *the* central role. Yet the Q3 2020 Unstuck Church Report revealed that only 21 percent of church leaders agreed that they have a "well-defined digital ministry strategy to engage with people who are outside the church and outside the faith." Which means, of course, that almost 80 percent don't.[3]

OPENING THE DIGITAL FRONT DOOR

More than thirty years ago, I wrote a book titled *Opening the Front Door: Worship and Church Growth*, for the Convention Press of the Southern Baptist Convention (SBC). The thesis was simple but, for the time, provocative: the front door of the church was no longer Sunday school but the weekend service. For decades, Sunday school had been enshrined as the front door of the church, the church's evangelistic engine, and the experience to which members invited people to attend. But my research of the SBC showed that beginning in 1971, more people were attending the weekend service than Sunday school. Further, the weekend service was the starting point for exploring the church. Visitors didn't begin with Sunday school, they began with the weekend worship service.

Though it's essential that we keep the weekend-service door open, the primary front door of the church has changed again. It's no longer the weekend service but an online experience. Whether it's a visit to a website or an online campus, the front door is digital. If I were to write a similar book today, I would title it *Opening the Digital Front Door*.

Here are the new assumptions that come with this revelation: First, people want to check a church out online before attending in person, just like they want to check everything else out first online. Second, they may attend or view online for months before visiting in person (if they visit at all). Third, they want to interact online. Finally, they are accustomed to being served digitally in almost every way.

It doesn't matter whether you like these four assumptions or even agree with them. They characterize our mission field, and we will either engage people how they want to be engaged or we will fail to reach them for Christ. This is the only way the vast majority will even consider being engaged. We will either open that front door or leave it firmly closed to them.

So how do we open the new front door to people? It begins by embracing how they are willing to explore the Christian faith (not to mention your church), their preferred systems of delivery (how they want to receive what you have to offer), and the new nature of communication through social media. Your church's relationship with the unchurched now begins online.

> ### DIGITAL FRONT DOOR ASSUMPTIONS
>
> 1. People want to check a church out online before attending in person.
> 2. They may attend or view online for months before visiting in person.
> 3. They want to be able to interact online.
> 4. They are accustomed to being served digitally in almost every way.

This raises an important question: How do you create an online presence that removes unnecessary barriers to full online exploration and engagement? We are used to thinking of barriers to in-person weekend services, such as style (music and architecture), comfort (casual dress), accessibility of the message (contemporary translation of the Bible), and cultural relevance (sermon topics, use of film or drama). Are those barriers relevant to digital exploration? Yes and no. Most still are because part of people's exploration, if you engage them, includes viewing a service or a message online or listening to a podcast. But digital exploration is so much more, and the barriers we need to remove are so much more involved.

The biggest barrier is if you don't even have a digital presence: you don't have a website, aren't on social media, don't offer your services or messages online, and don't use digital media to reach out. The majority of individuals who come to an in-person service for the first time have already explored the church online. If you are not online to allow that exploration, you have closed your front door. Don't expect them to come in person.

But let's assume you have a digital front door, whether it is a website, social media, or both. Here are some questions about just how open your door is. Who is your website designed to serve? For most churches, it is designed for the members and active attenders of the church. What about your Facebook page? Is that for your church community or for those who might be exploring your church? What about your Instagram account? Twitter feed? It's not that you can't make posts related to the life of your church or that your website can't serve up information necessary for your church community. But what will reading it and seeing it be like for someone who is not a part of your church family? What about someone who is not a Christian but may be open to exploring or trying to understand the Christian faith?

The point is to think of your digital presence as your front door. Is your website's homepage for the first-time guest? Are the primary links designed to serve someone exploring your church digitally? Is your Facebook page inviting and monitored, serving those who post questions? Is what you post on Instagram engaging and intriguing? If someone clicks and scrolls their way through your online presence, is there something that makes them stay and click and scroll further instead of moving on to something else? They will give you only a handful of seconds. According to research by Microsoft, the average attention span dropped from 12 seconds in 2000 to just 8 seconds in 2015.[4] Think about your in-person events. You have signage, greeters, and welcome areas, and create an atmosphere and experience designed to serve the needs of first-time guests. You should take just as much care with your online presence.

At Mecklenburg Community Church, we put an enormous amount of research and intentionality into our website (www.mecklenburg.org). The main page is designed for a first-time guest. When you land on the page, you are met by all of the information you need to find out more about the church. Main tabs include "Attend," "Connect," "Serve," and the "More Info" button that will immediately link you to some of the history of the church. Links to our next live event and the online campus are prominent. Beyond this are ways to follow and stay connected through social media. The goal is simple: the website is not simply the front door but the first impression.

THE IMPORTANCE OF SOCIAL MEDIA

The World Economic Forum has revealed that of all the things people use social media for, the use that has increased the most (by more than 30 percent) is shopping. People have been going online to explore products for a while, but increasingly they are doing so through social media. The study found that 64 percent of Generation Z and 62 percent of millennials say that they use social channels for product research or that social channels influence their purchasing.[5]

In our world, evangelism is primarily conducted not door to door but medium to medium, specifically social media, and especially visually driven social media. The most popular site in 2021 was not Google but TikTok. Joining TikTok in the list of most popular sites were Instagram and YouTube.[6] The influence of YouTube cannot be overstated. A 2017 study found that when asked how they wanted to learn something,

Gen Zers' number-one answer was YouTube. Ninety-five percent of all teens watch it and say they can't live without it. Along with TikTok, it's the primary way they get their news. It's the number-one place they go to be entertained, and it's the top go-to for shopping recommendations.[7] A survey of more than a thousand children between the ages of six and seventeen by the travel company First Choice found that nearly 75 percent now want a career in online videos. More than a third wanted to be a YouTuber, and nearly a fifth wanted to work as a vlogger. It's not about the money. The top attractions were "creativity, fame and the opportunity for self-expression."[8] According to Internet Matters, more than four out of ten children are uploading videos to the web by the time they reach fifteen years old.[9]

So what does this mean for the church? Here are six simple ways to begin using YouTube to open your digital front door:

1. *Start a YouTube Channel.* It's increasingly common for churches of all sizes to self-produce videos for use in weekend services, student ministry, and children's ministry. Why not start your own YouTube channel for those videos? Or even better, develop multiple channels: one for your children's ministry, another for your music team, and another for weekend messages. Such channels not only reinforce what, say, a child learned on the weekend but are an easy way for them to share what they've learned with their friends.

2. *Use YouTube Videos.* When permission is available, use existing YouTube videos. If the most popular form of communication and discourse is visual and is housed on platforms like YouTube, then why wouldn't you use what people are viewing and talking about when appropriate? Viral videos can be used as sermon illustrations, as talking points, and even to demonstrate a point of view you disagree with. We live in a day when the visual is the primary mode of discourse, so if you can "show" an idea instead

of "tell" it, go for show every time. YouTube videos can even be used as entertaining ice breakers for broaching a topic. I once did a series titled "Viral Verses" on verses that were trending, were the most downloaded, or were the most viewed, and how so often they are taken out of context. I opened each week with a look at a comedic video that was going viral at that moment as a way of talking about all things viral and then specifically about the viral verses. It was a simple but effective cultural touchpoint.[10]

3. *Develop YouTube-Style Videos.* When you develop videos (and churches of all sizes can do this with today's readily accessible and inexpensive technology), consider the kinds of videos that are popular on YouTube. Most are not polished, but they do have identifiable styles and cuts, angles and vibes. Our children's ministry team tracks the most popular YouTube channels for children to stay abreast of style and then develops videos in similar fashion as a cultural bridge. Some of the most viewed videos on YouTube are for children, including the most watched YouTube video of all time, "Baby Shark," which was the first video to be watched more than ten billion times.[11] For adults, think of the enormous popularity of DIY videos and TED talks. Take cues from what's clearly popular when you develop your own. Again, the production values are often low, but the content and engagement are high.

4. *Study YouTube Videos Culturally.* Because we are such a visual culture and YouTube is currently the primary platform for videos, study YouTube culturally. Consider it "Missiology 101." Here's what I suggest you look for: (1) topics that seem to be of interest, (2) how people communicate, both stylistically and verbally, (3) what the most popular videos are and what their themes seem to be, and (4) the thinking reflected in the videos that you can either take advantage of or must develop apologetics to counter. It's all too common to assume we know what people

are thinking and feeling, asking and questioning. There's no need to assume when YouTube's most popular videos can give you a quick education.

5. *YouTube Your Website.* Next, YouTube your website. Fewer people today will read an ad; they are, however, more likely to watch one. They may not read a movie review, but they'll watch a short trailer. Is your website video based or article based? If it's article based, move away from extensive writing and instead use numerous short videos that present information about your church—emphasis on short. If visitors see that a video is going to last thirty-seven minutes, chances are they will pass. If they see it takes two minutes or less, they will be much more likely to watch it. That's the appeal of TikTok and one of the reasons it has been downloaded billions of times worldwide.[12] TikTok allows users to post videos that are one minute or less.

> ### THE CHURCH AND YOUTUBE
>
> 1. Start a YouTube channel.
> 2. Use YouTube videos.
> 3. Develop YouTube-style videos.
> 4. Study YouTube videos culturally.
> 5. YouTube your website.
> 6. YouTube your evangelism.

An entire subgenre known as Christian TikTok exists, where Christian influencers publish everything from sermonettes to best Bible study practices. And many of the young content creators "are on a mission to spark revival among Generation Z."[13] But that, of course, is what any church can do as well.

6. *YouTube Your Evangelism.* At Mecklenburg Community Church, the church I have pastored for more than thirty years, we crafted a series of fifteen or so YouTube videos that raise, and then attempt to answer, the top questions people have about the Christian faith. Shorter is more engaging, so we made fifteen videos instead of just

one—one video per question. There is no end to the number, style, content, and intent of evangelistically oriented videos you can create and post.

Once you've opened your digital front door, you're going to have to be ready to affirm the people who walk through it.

THE IMPORTANCE OF AFFIRMING ONLINE ENGAGEMENT

In March 2020, most churches rushed not only to be online but also to create as much of an online presence as possible and to encourage any and all online engagement. Lifeway Research found that 45 percent of Americans say they watched a church service online during the COVID-19 pandemic, including many who said they didn't normally attend in person. As Scott McConnell, executive director of Lifeway Research, noted, "A form of communication that was not even used by most churches before the pandemic has now reached almost half of Americans."[14]

After that, people expected churches to have an ongoing, robust online presence. They even expected to be able to attend church online after in-person services resumed. Why wouldn't they? In the minds of many, if not most, people, the church had finally embraced the digital world. Sadly, not all churches seized the cultural moment. Instead, once they reopened, some churches greatly diminished, if not ended, their online presence, discouraged anything digital as not being real church, and even shamed people for not attending in person.

That was a tactical mistake that willfully ignored what had happened in our world. There's no going back from the necessary online engagement that was accelerated during the pandemic. As a cable news report proclaimed,

Church, as we've known it for the past few generations, is over. Every church you've ever attended, or that you drive by on your way to a Sunday sporting event, was built on a physical attendance model that is location-centric.

As a result, church leaders and pastors have spent time every week encouraging, inviting, and pleading with people to come to a specific place at a specific time on Sundays. This approach has created church staffing models, systems, and ministry strategies focused on improving attendance. It's also why there is an annual Top 100 list of America's most attended churches.

But that way of doing church is dead.[15]

While that model is not truly dead (yet), people will naturally vacillate between online and in-person offerings—between the virtual and physical—from this point on, feeling that both options are not only acceptable but also count as having *attended*. This hybrid model is the model all churches must embrace. Let's not have cyber wars the way we had worship wars. It's not about whether churches should be in person or online; they should be both.

And we are learning, most notably from the State of the Bible survey, that people who attend churches with both in-person and online service options have a more positive opinion of their church experience than attenders at churches with only one option. Those who attended both in person and online were most likely to strongly agree (44 percent) that their church services increased their desire to read the Bible. The same results were found when respondents were asked about whether church services increased their understanding of Scripture. Churches offering both online and in-person services found higher percentages strongly agreeing that, indeed, they had.[16] The good news is that even after almost every church was back to meeting in person, Hartford Institute for Religion Research found in 2021 that eight in ten US churches were continuing to provide hybrid services, offering both in-person and online options.[17]

People will choose based on their desired experience, readiness to surface physically, and, even among core members, how their week went. Rather than fight this change, embrace it. It will not prove helpful to elevate in-person attendance over online attendance, much less shame online attenders. The better and more strategic path is to embrace any and all engagement. As Carey Nieuwhof has written,

> The hybrid-church model will simply become church. In other words, hosting church online and in person is just how you do church to reach the next generation.
>
> People have lived in the slipstream of digital and in-real-life for well over a decade now, and church leaders will realize that church online is both a necessity and an opportunity.
>
> It's good that the debate over online church will fade into the background because then leaders can get on with the key task: Reaching people however they come to you—in person or online.[18]

One of the most strategic decisions I made as a leader, and this was just prior to COVID, was to affirm that attending in person or online was *attending*. When COVID hit, this proved to be pivotal. Our experience has been that when you provide a combination of in-person and online experiences and events and give people the freedom to sample and choose, overall engagement goes up exponentially. At the time of this writing, our online campus is where, by far, the greatest number of people attend and the arena for our greatest growth. Our in-person weekend services are still running below prepandemic levels. Yet select in-person events—Christmas services, fall experiences—see record numbers. Being okay with that is critical to the new reality.

The goal is to become omnichannel, allowing individuals to connect online and offline seamlessly. In retail, becoming omnichannel involves driving traffic to stores through services like "buy online and pickup in store (BOPIS)," as well as offering "an expanded set of ship-from-store services."[19] As Dave Anderson has written, "An omnichannel approach to church would allow people to fully connect and engage with a church without the need to step inside a physical environment every week. They could attend one Sunday, listen to the message on podcast the following week, watch a live online stream the Sunday after, and catch the message on demand in a church app the week after that."

He notes that this "shifts the church from a location-centric approach to an audience-centric approach that allows people to connect and engage with churches both digitally *and* physically."[20] Every church should embrace the new reality: You have at least two campuses. One is physical, and one is digital.

And when I say "campus," I do mean campus.

Planting Online

Space: the final frontier. These are the
voyages of the starship Enterprise. Its five-
year mission: to explore strange new worlds.
To seek out new life and new civilizations. To
boldly go where no man has gone before!
—OPENING MONOLOGUE, ORIGINAL STAR TREK SERIES[1]

I am a wholehearted believer in church planting. In fact, I am a church planter. I planted Meck in October 1992 and have served as its pastor ever since. I don't know of a single missiologist who doesn't give the same answer for the future vitality of the church: we must plant new churches! I couldn't agree more. Of keen interest to anyone wanting to plant a church or support church planting in general is pinpointing areas of need: fast-growing areas, underchurched areas, and sectors of our world where the numbers of unchurched people are high. This is why it is stunning to me that the key place to plant a church—where the need is greatest and the "fields white unto harvest"—is almost entirely overlooked. I'm talking about planting a church online. Or at the very least, planting a campus of your church online. And notice I said "campus." There is a difference between being online and having a digital campus of your church online.

So what does an online campus entail? First, what an online campus is not: it is not a Facebook stream of your in-person weekend service; it is not a video of your weekend service parked on YouTube; it is not a livestream of your in-person service that people can watch through your website.

An online campus is a digital campus that is akin to a physical campus in every possible way. The main difference between a physical campus and an online campus is that it exists, and is engaged, digitally. It has set service times that you attend and where you are greeted by hosts. There are pastors ready to meet you and engage with you. It is staffed in almost every way you would staff a physical campus. You are introduced to online opportunities for children's ministry and adult classes and invited to attend select in-person events.

An online campus is critical to fostering a sense of not only engagement but community. During a recent Church and Culture Conference,[2] when one of our online campus staff was asked why we offer set service times instead of just posting the service online for random viewing, she answered:

> This is really [all about] community. If you're sitting in your living room by yourself, you may not really feel as though you are [experiencing] community. And if you have a question, you may not know where to go.
>
> I think having a staff member online who is the "face" of the campus—the name of someone who you can come back to week after week—is great.
>
> They can answer your questions and you feel as though you are connected with them. You *are* connected with them actually—it's not just a feeling.[3]

The service has been prepared specifically for online consumption and engagement—not just what is said but also how it is filmed and presented. This makes the service different from the in-person service. For example, it is shorter—online attention spans are shorter than in-person attention spans. At Meck, instead of sixty to sixty-five minutes for a service, which is what our in-person services typically run, our online campus service averages around forty to forty-five minutes. Our announcements segments are tailored for online consumption, online engagement, and online attenders. When we talk about serving opportunities, we don't highlight anything related to serving during an in-person service. Instead, we highlight online serving opportunities, or serving days and events that are outside of weekend service times. While the creative elements, including music, might borrow from what is also being prepared for the in-person service, they are presented and filmed differently for online consumption and with the understanding that we are attempting to connect with a single person or a very small group of people such as a family.

My message is the same, but it too is filmed and presented differently. I'm filmed in a studio, sitting instead of standing, talking directly into the camera. It is much more intimate—as if I'm having a conversation with just the person watching. We have had groups of people numbering in the twenties, thirties, and even sixties engaging our online campus in places such as a local brewery or over lunch in an office conference room, but we know that the average viewer is a single person or a couple, maybe an entire family, but that's it. And just in case you're wondering, Barna Research found that about two-thirds of those who have engaged with online services (67 percent) say they are learning just as much from a streamed sermon as from an in-person sermon.[4]

It's so important that a service for a digital campus is designed for online consumption. Early on in our online offerings, we didn't do this, but it was a game changer when we did. One of my sons was in a conversation with a group of men in our church (both of my sons are pastors at our church), and one of the men had some interesting things to say about when we first made the transition from showing a recording of our in-person weekend service online to crafting an experience solely for our online campus. I'm going to have to paraphrase what my son relayed to me, but this is the essence of what he said:

> In years past, I visited the online campus from time to time, and it was okay. I mean, it was one of the weekend services filmed and put online. It wasn't as good as being there. And you could tell the sound and mixing wasn't the best for internet consumption. It couldn't be—it wasn't filmed or designed for the internet. It was a captured live event. You also knew you were watching a filmed service. The message was being given to that service's crowd. Now granted, it was about as good of a filmed service as you could watch. But man, I love what we're doing now. Everything about it assumes that I'm watching it like I am—online! The sound and light and mix are perfect for the internet. The creativity of the worship and the arts, the nature of the presentation, the way the message is given as if just to me! I mean, it's like he's talking directly to me!

I had a similar conversation with a long-time attender who told me, almost as a confession, that he preferred the online campus to in-person services. He loved that online, he can spread out his Bible and notes on a table, pour a good cup of coffee, and engage in a way he couldn't have before. And it goes without saying what a difference having an online campus makes for someone who has physical or mental challenges or is immunocompromised.

The whole idea behind an online campus is that when people sign on and then later sign off, they feel they have attended a service. *Experienced* a service. After a service has ended, they feel they have just been with their church home and their community, because for them, that *was* their church home. That *is* their community. These people would tell you that they attend Meck and that Meck is their church home, even though they may have never darkened the doorstep of our physical campus.

The other day, someone in one of the chat rooms during an online campus service said they were asked at work where they went to church. They said, "Meck." The person said, "Oh, where is that?" to which they responded, "Honestly, I don't know. I've never been there. But it's my church!" And with an online campus, the goal is not to get them to transition to physical attendance. We make it clear that everyone should attend whatever campus is best for them on any given week. For some, it's a hybrid—sometimes online, sometimes in person. For the vast majority—and I do mean the *vast* majority—they are content to have the online campus as their church home.

THE THEOLOGY OF AN ONLINE CAMPUS

I am sure many biblical and theological questions are racing through your mind about affirming online engagement instead of in person. There is little doubt it stretches our thinking about ecclesiology (the doctrine of the church). Pastor and author John MacArthur has been publicly dismissive of such ventures, stating that a service held online does not count as genuine church, even going so far as to say it goes against the biblical definition of proper worship. "It's not church. It's watching TV," he has maintained. "There's nothing about that that fulfills the biblical definition of coming together, stimulating one another to love and good works, coming together. . . . We are only the church when we are together."[5] I respectfully disagree. Though MacArthur wants to hold high the value of many embodied aspects of communal life, his referencing the passage in Hebrews and asserting that we are only the church when we are in person is, in my view, both misguided and misinformed.

First, let's deal with Scripture, specifically the Hebrews passage, which says, "And let us consider how we may spur one another on toward love and good deeds, not giving up meeting together, as some are in the habit of doing, but encouraging one another—and all the more as you see the Day approaching" (Heb. 10:24–25). Many people conclude that this passage mandates meeting in Christian community for in-person worship services.

There is little doubt that we are to be worshipers, both public and private, and that one of the marks of the early church was gathering to do just that (Acts 2:42–47). But this was not what the author of Hebrews was mandating. The author wasn't talking about gathering for corporate worship or for any church event. Instead, the author of Hebrews was speaking about not giving up on relationships, of not giving up on people. He was issuing a clarion call to be faithful to relationships with other Christians. This passage is about the importance of Christians spurring one another on, encouraging one another, and doing so in a world that demands perseverance.

That this is the meaning is heightened further by the Greek word translated "giving up," which is used for *desertion* and *abandonment*. This passage says don't abandon each other relationally; you need each other's support. It is the same word Paul used when writing to Timothy about Paul's being deserted by Demas (2 Tim. 4:10) and then a few sentences later about his being deserted when no one came to support him at his first defense (2 Tim. 4:16). Paul also used it in his second letter to the Corinthians when speaking of being "hard pressed on every side, but not crushed; perplexed, but not in despair; persecuted, but not abandoned" (2 Cor. 4:8–9). Perhaps most to the point, it was the word Jesus uttered when he felt abandoned by the Father during his crucifixion (Matt. 27:46). In every case, the issue was the betrayal of a relational commitment that left another feeling abandoned.

The point of the Hebrews passage is that we should not pull back from engaging one another relationally in ways that stir us on to greater levels of love and good works, to never fail in being like iron against iron sharpening one another (Prov. 27:17). Author David Croteau calls making this passage about compulsory in-person, public worship services one of the great urban legends of the New Testament.[6] The passage is more about keeping an appointment with a friend in need at a Starbucks than it is about going to a church service.

FINDING A DIGITAL COUNTERPART

Second, let's challenge ourselves to consider that not everything we used to do in person has to be done in person—even the relational commitment the author of Hebrews is calling for. I can support and encourage someone virtually as well as physically, unless their need is a physical one. We need to be careful not to make normative how we've always done things. It's a mistake to assume that if we have always done something in person, it must only ever be done in person. We can say to younger generations, "You can't do community online," but they will only retort, "Well, sorry to tell you this, but you can, and we do."

We must ruthlessly evaluate whether everything we have done in person might just have a digital counterpart or manifestation. You might be surprised how often it does. For years now, long before COVID, almost every human was living a hybrid life shifting between digital and real interactions. It has simply been accelerated of late. As Carey Nieuwhof has written, "You text your friend one second, pivot to a YouTube video the next to get a recipe for dinner, and then meet your family in the kitchen to cut some vegetables for the meal. For years now, you've moved seamlessly between the digital and the real. Church will be that way in the future too, which is why the hybrid church—offering both digital and physical ministry—is here to stay. People will be in the building one week, watching solo online the next, and the third gathering with some friends in a home or (better yet) serving in the community to *be* the church."[7]

Another dynamic is how much is made of how distracting our world has become, largely through digital media. One of the concerns about an online service is that there will be even more distractions taking away from worship or biblical teaching. That while watching, you will be tempted to go to the bathroom, check email, or visit another site. Then you might be distracted by a text or be interrupted by a child. Without a doubt, this can be the case for some people. Yet we have found through our online campus services that the opposite is true. The majority of people are watching when their children are asleep or napping. (We schedule some of our services with that in mind.)[8] They are alone and engaged, often watching on large screen TVs. When asked during the Church and Culture Conference about the issue of distraction, here is how our online campus director responded:

> [Removing distractions is] one of the things that we try to do here in the auditorium, and for our in-person services it takes us multiple songs to get people to let down their defenses because they're analyzing the room.
>
> They're feeling weird about singing or reacting emotionally to what's happening because there's somebody sitting right next to them who they don't know.
>
> When you're by yourself, you can go higher up and deeper in much faster, and you can sustain that much longer. That song—all of a sudden, you're there from start to end instead of checking out because a baby cried or something. When you're engaging it alone, it just allows you to do a different thing.

So in person, it might take us twenty-five minutes to get people focused on what we're doing and get to their hearts, but that happens so much faster online. Without the in-person distractions, we can just get there faster and go deeper online.[9]

VIRTUAL MISSION FIELD

But a website, social media, and an online campus should not be our only forays into a digital post-Christian world. We should enter the virtual mission field. At the time of this writing, according to Statista, it is estimated that there are 3.24 billion gamers worldwide, which is about 40 percent of the world's population. Writing for *Outreach* magazine, Jonathan Sprowl asks, "What is the church doing to reach these people whose lives are increasingly lived online?"[10] Or as David Roach titled an article for *Christianity Today*, "The Next Mission Field Is a Game."[11] Generation Z and Generation Alpha, says *AdAge*, are "growing up in virtual worlds in a way no previous generation has—with Fortnite and Roblox going mainstream and blockchain technologies" making waves. *AdAge* adds, "The metaverse has been set up to scratch the itch of socialization in a way that didn't exist until this moment."[12]

In June 2016, D. J. Soto purchased his first virtual-reality headset. Then he discovered AltSpaceVR, a virtual-reality meeting space. He soon envisioned planting a church in a virtual environment. On the Sunday he held his first service, five people showed up, one of whom was an atheist from Denmark. From that point on, Soto knew he could potentially reach anyone in the world with the message of Christ in virtual-reality environments.[13] Joining Soto in AltspaceVR is Life. Church, which in late 2021 announced it would be hosting services on the virtual-reality platform, offering its first services in December of that year. "While critics might question if real connections can be made in the metaverse, Life.Church has seen countless lives changed through relationships in digital spaces over the years," said spokeswoman Rachel Feuerborn. In the church's experience, she said, people "are often more willing to let their guard down and have deep, meaningful conversations more quickly from the safety of anonymity than they are face-to-face."[14]

Not only can virtual-reality environments extend our reach but the metaverse can offer enhanced virtual-reality experiences. New environments can be created to allow participants to explore various aspects of the biblical story. They can cross the Red Sea as the Israelites did, experience a storm at sea as the apostle Paul did, or walk the streets of Jerusalem. "It's a 360-degree immersive experience that brings the Bible to life," notes Sprowl. An additional benefit is the safety of the environment: "because everyone interacts with one another through avatars, a range of people from every faith to no-faith backgrounds feels comfortable participating in virtual small group discussions, where they can examine Christianity in a safe environment."[15]

Jason Poling, lead pastor of Cornerstone Church in Yuba City, California, began ministry in the metaverse in 2019. He too discovered that many people were willing to have a spiritual conversation within the first five minutes. The anonymity made people much more comfortable to ask deeper questions sooner. Ministry in the virtual world is also critical to reach people in younger demographics, such as Generation Z and Generation Alpha. Consider that the livestreaming platform Twitch, where participants of various games talk with each other as they play, has an estimated fifteen million daily users, of which 73 percent are under the age of thirty-five.[16]

I know of one member of our church who is active on Twitch and uses it to direct people to our online campus, and then, through Twitch, watches a service with them. He has a following in a unique interest group that has nothing to do with spiritual things, but through that shared interest and his expertise in it, he and his followers have both a relationship and trust. He just casually mentions that if anyone wants to join him as he watches Meck's online campus, much the way they join him to watch him pursue their shared interest, he would welcome the time together. Many do.

Chicago-based NewThing, a ministry of Community Christian Church, is launching a digital church-planting campaign it hopes will result in hundreds of new churches. "The plan is to start looking at digital space and the metaverse," says Jeff Reed, director of NewThing's digital realm, "as communities where people are gathering." The goal is to capitalize on the "increasing number of people who have wide social networks that exist entirely online."[17]

As with an online campus, questions of ecclesiology arise with the metaverse, particularly the degree to which physical interaction is necessary for there to truly be "church" or to be a participant in the body of Christ. But we've wrestled with such questions before in response to a changing spiritual climate or an advance in technology and eventually determined the use of technology was both theologically acceptable and missionally decisive. Corrina Laughlin, who teaches media studies at Loyola Marymount University, has studied evangelicals' use of media and technology. She notes that evangelicals have long been early adopters of new tech, and not just recently. She points out that early in American evangelicalism, preachers like Charles Fuller and Aimee Semple McPherson took full advantage of radio. Billy Graham embraced television for his crusades and even founded a film studio, World Wide Pictures, in 1953. Then came the televangelists of the 1980s and the contemporary Christian musicians of the '90s. "In the digital era, evangelicals have continued to embrace media technologies as they have entered the zeitgeist," she writes, "[using] the technologies of secular culture to spread their own message and values."[18] In an article for the *Atlantic*, Laughlin quotes Tom Pounder, the online-campus pastor at New Life Christian Church in Chantilly, Virginia: "Online ministry is here to stay, and the churches that don't invest in this area won't be."[19]

Rethinking Delivery

*The truth is, no online data base will replace
your daily newspaper. . . . [It has been predicted]
that we'll soon buy books and newspapers
straight over the Internet. Uh, sure. . . . We're
promised instant catalog shopping—just
point and click for great deals. We'll order
airline tickets over the network. . . . Stores
will become obsolete. So how come my local
mall does more business in an afternoon than
the entire Internet handles in a month?*
—CLIFFORD STOLL, "THE INTERNET? BAH!" (1995)[1]

More than thirty years ago, Melvin Kranzberg, a professor of the history of technology at Georgia Institute of Technology, laid out six laws of technology based on tensions and geopolitical realities resulting from the Cold War. They have become legendary among technologists, serving as something of a Hippocratic oath for all people who build things—so much so that in 2017, the *Wall Street Journal* outlined their ongoing relevance.[2] One of Kranzberg's laws is, "Invention is the mother of necessity." No, you didn't read that wrong. The tried-and-true phrase is, "Necessity is the mother of invention." But the point, Kranzberg wrote, is that "every technical innovation seems to require additional technical advances in order to make it fully effective."[3]

Which brings us to delivery systems.

DELIVERY SYSTEMS

When is the last time you thought about delivery systems? If you are in the world of commerce, you probably answered, "Today." It's one of the most pressing concerns facing the marketplace, where invention has become the mother of necessity. A recent report found that COVID-19 has accelerated the shift to ecommerce by at least five years.[4] Some say it has accelerated things by as many as fifteen years.[5]

A delivery system is simply the way you deliver a product or a message. Leadership has been described as getting from "here to there." But a delivery system is how you get "this to there." One might assume delivery systems don't require much thought, but that would be wrong and for one simple reason: the way people want and need things to be delivered has changed. For example, try to go out and buy a CD at a store. Vinyl albums are having a retro moment, but not CDs. Today, the primary way Americans listen to music is through a streaming service. While once CD players were standard in new vehicles, car companies don't even offer them anymore. If you insist on trying to deliver your music through CDs, you will deliver very little.[6]

Now think about training. In just a handful of years, the entire world of training (at least in the corporate world) has evolved from a "one-size-fits-all approach driven by instructor-led training, to more personalized learning that happens in the flow of work, accessible 24/7."[7]

Think about traditional education. A report from Education Design

Lab found that if universities and colleges want to stay relevant, they will move online. They will "adopt new ways to deliver academic materials, focusing on customizable courses and experiences outside of the class-room."[8] They'll move to a Netflix-style distribution of course materials.

Here are the four models of delivery that Education Design Lab projects colleges will adopt in the future:[9]

1. *Platform Facilitator.* From online content to food orders, Generation Z has become accustomed to customizable consumption, and education may follow. Some universities may begin to offer a Netflix-style distribution of course materials, while others will be "content providers for those platforms, licensing courses, experiences, certificates and other services," according to the report. Many university administrators are already considering the idea of building AI-enabled programs to distribute academic videos, according to a 2018 survey by Sonic Foundry's Mediasite and University Business.[10]

2. *Experiential Curator.* Institutions that adopt this model will take advantage of advanced data analytics tools and videoconferencing to expand their academic offerings beyond the classroom walls, according to the report. Experiential curators will use "advances in assessment, the maturation of online and hybrid education and the increasingly connected globe to provide, measure and certify transformative experiences outside the classroom."[11]

3. *Learning Certifier.* Universities embracing this model will pair mobile technology with data dashboards where students can accrue microcredentials, in some ways gamifying the higher education system, the report's writers note. Experiences outside the classroom, including extracurricular activities and internships, can be collected and marked off within the dashboard to provide future employers with evidence of graduates' educational experiences that could make them well-rounded employees.

4. *Workforce Integrator.* Workforce integrators establish corporate partnerships to build curricula and offer extracurricular activities, such as hackathons, where students can build connections with future employers. These collaborations will also ensure students graduate with the skills needed to fill jobs in specific fields.

"Rather than simply change the delivery model or launch new programs and supports, we wanted to help institutions understand the pace of labor market changes and student needs as we stand on the precipice of artificial intelligence–enabled, full-on digital competency–based learning," write the report's authors.[12]

I'll admit, that quote's a bit too techie. So let's translate it. Think about seminaries. They can deliver theological education through a three-year residential program at a bricks-and-mortar school as they have for almost all of their history, or they can offer online education and degrees. There is little doubt that the three-year residential program has many benefits, but, like the CD, it isn't how many people listen to their educational music anymore, so to speak.

> **ONLINE EDUCATIONAL DELIVERY ROLES**
>
> 1. Platform Facilitator
> 2. Experiential Curator
> 3. Learning Certifier
> 4. Workforce Integrator

Today, graduate students are often older, and, because of family and economic responsibilities, many need to pursue graduate degrees on a part-time basis and probably are not able to uproot and relocate to another city. Yes, a seminary can go multisite, but as Fuller, Moody, and other seminaries have learned, multisite is just an extension of the residential bricks-and-mortar model, not a truly new delivery system. (They've now closed many of the physical sites they had opened.) Online is simply how and where most people want to learn. It dominates every other educational tributary into their lives, from TED Talks to Google searches, online DIY tutorials to YouTube instructional videos.

If seminaries don't rethink their delivery systems, they might not have anyone to deliver their education to.

The same is true for churches. Increasing numbers of people are downloading and listening to podcasts, watching online services, and taking online courses. Are you delivering discipleship and instruction solely in antiquated ways? There's no need to remind me of the importance of touch in a high-tech world or that spiritual formation can never be fully achieved virtually; I agree there is much that should remain life on life—doing life with others. But is there no role at all for digital learning or digital discipleship? Let's dig deeper into what changes in education might mean for the church.

COLLEGES ARE HAVING TO CHANGE; SO WILL YOU

In 2018, the *New York Times* reported how the newest students—Generation Z—are transforming the way schools serve and educate. Bottom line? Generation Z is "super connected. But on their terms."[13] They do not tend to read books. They rarely read emails. They are a generation that "breathes through social media . . . sending presidents and deans to Instagram and Twitter." Further, students today want to navigate campus life on their own, getting food or help "when it is convenient for them. And, yes, on their mobile devices or phones." As the associate director of learning programs at Ohio State University notes, "It's not really technology to them." He's right. The iPhone came out when most students were in grade school, so to them, technology is just the natural way to live. So now schools such as Ohio State issue iPads, have courses designated "iPad required," and are building an app that "in addition to maps and bus routes has a course planner, grades, schedules and a Get Involved feature displaying student organizations." More customization is coming. Soon, when students open the app, it will know "which campus they are enrolled at, their major and which student groups they belong to."[14]

But higher education is experiencing not simply a communication revolution. Generation Z is forcing course makeovers, "pushing academics to be more hands-on and job-relevant." Millennials may have wanted climbing walls and en suite kitchens; Generation Z wants all things career development. Generation Z is even changing office hours. One journalism professor not only takes attendance via Twitter and posts assignments on Slack but holds office hours at 10:00 p.m. via the video conference site Zoom, "because that is when they have questions."[15] The only role email plays is during instruction on how to write a proper one as a business skill.

Another dynamic, new to mainstream academia, is how individualistic Generation Z students are and how individualistically they expect to be treated. They have been raised in a world of "tailored analytics" that instantly customizes their online experience. This leads them to expect that everything put in front of them will be customized. They do not like to learn in groups. They "like to think about information, then be walked through it to be certain they have it right." They want a model, and then to practice it. And while they very much favor videos over static content (remember the Pearson report that found that YouTube was their preferred learning method), they still want visual, face-to-face communication over texting. They are not always good at live social interaction, but they crave it. "They want authenticity and transparency," says Corey Seemiller, professor at Wright State University. "They like the idea of human beings being behind things."[16]

RETHINKING DELIVERY

What might this mean for the church? This may sound repetitive, but perhaps that is good:

1. Embrace social media and the technology that facilitates it, and then use it as much as you can to communicate, inform, and serve as you encourage people to take next steps in spiritual formation.
2. As much as you can, customize what you offer.
3. Be practical in your content. Consider foundational offerings on subjects such as how to read the Bible, how to pray, how to have a quiet time (or a time of devotion), and what it means to become a Christian.
4. Adjust to the schedule of the person you are trying to serve. This may involve offering on-demand courses.
5. Get visual in every way you can, particularly using video, but facilitate the delivery of the content and debrief in person.

Here's an example: We developed an online systematic-theology course. I wrote and taught the course, which was filmed over several weeks. The course ended up being seven installments of around forty-five minutes each. A workbook was created to go along with the course. Students enrolled and for seven weeks participated in the class during lunch hour. Though the teaching was a recording, I joined the class live to answer questions.

> **RETHINKING DELIVERY FOR THE CHURCH**
>
> 1. Embrace social media.
> 2. Customize what you have to offer.
> 3. Be practical in your content.
> 4. Adjust to changing schedules.
> 5. Get visual.

Digital learning is about far more than just tech. As Stephanie Morgan, director of learning solutions at Bray Leino Learning, summarizes it, "In reality, it's more a way of learning than any single type of learning, requiring an organisation-wide mindset shift to be truly successful."[17] Particularly in regard to self-directed learning. Research shows that "millennials and Generation Z want independent learning opportunities, taking control of their own learning to access what they want, when they need it. As younger generations are used to finding instant answers to everyday problems outside of work—think a YouTube video or 'how do I' Google search—they now expect similar responsiveness at work."[18]

THE NEW,
NEW COMMUNITY

It's a Lonely World

The most terrible poverty is loneliness
and the feeling of being unloved.
—MOTHER TERESA[1]

When Facebook, now Meta, reached the two billion user mark, and had more than one hundred million users in what CEO Mark Zuckerberg called "meaningful communities" within Groups on Facebook, Zuckerberg made it a goal to raise that second number to one billion. He said, "If we can do this, it will not only turn around the whole decline in community membership we've seen for decades, it will start to strengthen our social fabric and bring the world closer together." He then compared the site to a church, noting that "people who go to church are more likely to volunteer and give to charity—not just because they're religious, but because they're part of a community."[2] Commenting on Zuckerberg's remarks, Halee Gray Scott said, "Zuckerberg is right that Facebook has provided meaningful connections that the local church sometimes struggles to build among its disparate and busy members. While our newsfeeds may be filled with the highly polished versions of our friends' lives, groups from neighborhood networks to personality-type groups provide the opportunity to take the mask off and divulge our weaknesses and innermost thoughts. In the best cases, we rally around one another, support one another, pray for one another, and provide respect and space for various viewpoints."[3]

She added, though, that "Facebook, nor any other form of social media or any other form of organization, [can't] replace the church."[4] She's right. But that doesn't mean the church can't be served by social media, or that social media can't be served by the church, particularly in regard to community.

A LONELY WORLD

There are two realities about the changing nature of community in our digital world: First, it is largely in the digital world that community is established, and then that community often stays there. Studies even show that for people between the ages of thirteen and twenty-one, iPhone ownership is a prerequisite for social acceptance and engagement in social activity. As an eighteen-year-old high-school senior in New Jersey told a reporter, "If you don't have an iPhone, it's kind of frowned upon." A twenty-year-old sophomore at Rutgers University said, "If you don't have an iPhone, you're not getting added to group chats. That seems really mean, but it's difficult to group-text people if they don't have an iPhone."[5]

The second reality will seem strange, particularly in light of the first, and it's the persistence of loneliness, particularly within Generation Z. Global insurer Cigna, using the UCLA Loneliness Scale, polled twenty thousand Americans ages eighteen and older. The scale is a twenty-item questionnaire designed to gauge loneliness from twenty on the low end to eighty on the high end. Participants were asked how often they agreed with such prompts as "There is no one I can turn to" and "I feel part of a group of friends." Perhaps counterintuitively, seniors—those age seventy-two and older—scored lowest, meaning they are the least lonely of all the age groups. The national average was forty-four. Generation Z, or at least the segment that is ages eighteen to twenty-two, was the loneliest by far, collectively scoring a high of forty-eight.

This confirms what has been assumed by many—that the first generation raised in the context of social media is not being served socially at all. It's not that social media is isolating them further. (Heavy social-media users had only a slightly higher loneliness rating than those who never use social media.) It's just not helping them avoid loneliness. As Elizabeth Segal wrote in *Psychology Today*, "No matter how sophisticated we make the technology, it will *never* replace the feelings and connections of being physical with others face to face.... Today we see the desire for that physical connection. Coming through the forced isolation of the pandemic opened opportunities to be together in person, which is what people want and need. Being with others in person is the answer to building human connections. It can be aided but not replaced by technology."[6]

Jagdish Khubchandani, a health science professor at Ball State University, suggests that social media can provide a false sense of relief. Students attempt socialization on computers in their homes, leading them away from face-to-face interaction. "I have students who tell me they have 500 'friends,'" he notes, "but when they're in need, there's no one."[7] The research of Jean Twenge has found that the "number of teens who get together with their friends every day has been cut in half in just fifteen years, with especially steep declines recently."[8] This goes far beyond Generation Z. Three out of every ten millennials say they are always or often lonely. One out of every five say they have no friends at all.[9]

But this loneliness is not the result of the digital revolution. In his groundbreaking book *Bowling Alone*, Robert Putnam noted the loss of social capital in the world. As the title suggests, once we bowled in leagues, but now we bowl alone. Long before the internet became the wallpaper of our life (Putnam's book was released in 2000), there were already signs that we were a culture becoming increasingly disconnected from family, friends, neighbors, and other social structures. Putnam notes that as the nineteenth century turned into the twentieth, social capital was also at a low point. Urbanization, industrialization, and widespread immigration uprooted Americans from friends, social institutions, and families. New organizations were created to fill the need for social connection. His book argued that the need for new ways to connect was the same when the twentieth century turned into the twenty-first.[10] The church is uniquely poised, as it has always been, to provide just that.

> **THREE OUT OF EVERY TEN MILLENNIALS SAY THEY ARE ALWAYS OR OFTEN LONELY. ONE OUT OF EVERY FIVE SAY THEY HAVE NO FRIENDS AT ALL.**

THE NEW COMMUNITY

Nothing compares to the clearest picture of community that has ever been presented—of the *new* community, called together by Jesus. Few verses of Scripture capture that communal life better than Luke's record of the early church: "They devoted themselves to the apostles' teaching and to fellowship, to the breaking of bread and to prayer. Everyone was filled with awe at the many wonders and signs performed by the apostles. All the believers were together and had everything in common. They sold property and possessions to give to anyone who had need. Every day they continued to meet together in the temple courts. They broke bread in their homes and ate together with glad and sincere hearts, praising God and enjoying the favor of all the people. And the Lord added to their number daily those who were being saved" (Acts 2:42–47).

It has often been said that in this portrait, you find a communal life where you can love and be loved, know and be known, serve and be served, celebrate and be celebrated. Can this be achieved in a digital world? If so, can it have the depth and power to arrest the attention of a post-Christian world that is so desperately lonely?

Many voices contend that anything digital is the antithesis of community. As Jean Bethke Elshtain writes, "Cyberculture disconnects us from human communities in a particular temporal location sharing an actual physical space—even as it connects us in thin ways to strangers. These thin connections can be helpful if information is being shared, or human rights abuses reported, or medical technology being made available. But when the word *community* is used to describe what goes on in chat rooms, we realize . . . that the understanding of community is euphemistic in such a context. Real community means to be in relationship in the flesh."[11]

> **LESS THAN HALF OF ALL CHRISTIANS ACTIVE IN CHURCH SPEND TIME WITH OTHER BELIEVERS TO HELP THEM GROW IN THEIR FAITH. TWO-THIRDS SAY THEY DON'T NEED ANYONE IN THEIR LIVES TO HELP THEM WALK WITH GOD.**

Such sentiments are common in reflections about community and the digital revolution. In her work *Alone Together*, Sherry Turkle notes that "we are changed as technology offers us substitutes for connecting with each other face-to-face. . . . After an evening . . . in a networked game, we feel, at one moment, in possession of a full social life and, in the next, curiously isolated, in tenuous complicity with strangers."[12]

She then observes, "These days, being connected depends not on our distance from each other but from available communications technology. Most of the time, we carry that technology with us."[13] It's not that anyone celebrates "expecting more from technology and less from each other," Turkle's central point, but that is the reality of the people we are trying to reach and to draw into community.[14] An effort to pull someone into a deeper understanding of community with in-person dynamics will by necessity begin in the digital world.

As Felicia Wu Song notes, "Even though we desire connection, what we long for and are actually created for is something far deeper. What we actually need is communion."[15]

But the isolation and individualism of our world are not solved simply through an embodied community. A recent Lifeway study found that less than half of all Christians active in church spend time with other believers to help them grow in their faith.[16] The younger the age, the more individualistic a Christian is. Two-thirds say they don't need anyone in their lives to help them walk with God, which suggests that the need is not for less online community and more in-person community. We need to use every available means to foster community and then cast the biblical vision for going higher up and deeper in.

THE HYBRID COMMUNITY

In his book *Twenty-One Lessons for the Twenty-First Century*, Yuval Noah Harari describes what churches have to do "to bridge the chasm between online and offline." He writes, "A community may begin as an online gathering, but in order to truly flourish it will have to put down roots in the offline world too. . . . Physical communities have a depth that virtual communities cannot match, as least not in the near future. If I lie in bed sick at home in Israel, my online friends from California can talk to me, but they cannot bring me soup or a cup of tea."[17]

This is why a hybrid approach to community is so essential. There are severe drawbacks to community that is solely online, yet that is where most "community" is taking place. If we are going to bring someone offline and into real human interaction, into embodied community, we need to begin where they are, which means establishing and fostering online community. While that online community may exist in a diminished form compared with all that an embodied community can provide, to dismiss it entirely is counterproductive. It may not be all that someone needs from community, but it *is* a form of community. And it is very real for those who are experiencing it.

Like many pastors, I expected a rush back to church after the COVID-19 pandemic shuttered our church's doors. It didn't happen. It still hasn't happened. Many reasons have been offered to explain why: hesitancy because of health concerns; departures because of cultural and political divides arising during the pandemic; nominal attenders drifting into a more settled unchurched mode. But another reason receives too little attention: people *like* attending online as much as, if not more than, in person. And this is particularly so when a church has an effective online campus and encourages people to attend in the manner they desire. And before you think, *That's why you shouldn't have an online campus or encourage online attendance*, remember that without those two things, you would not have the engagement at all.

I recall having coffee with a long-term member of our church, someone mature in their faith and dedicated to the body of Christ. He told me he was surprised by how much he simply preferred attending online. He's not alone, and many would testify to finding real community there. In some ways, they are finding an even deeper and more meaningful community than they had experienced in person before. When our director of guest services was asked at the Church and Culture Conference what his biggest surprise was after reopening during the pandemic, this was his reply:

When we came back and started opening back up in person, I assumed that people were naturally going to come in waves.

That they would be thinking, "This is the best way to get that community that I've longed for." But what I was surprised by during all of that is the amount of community that was fostered amongst

COVID. As a pastor taking questions, I was surprised how deep the questions went so fast.

I can't tell you the number of conversations that I had with people that then led to a "Here's my email—I'd love to have a follow-up conversation about this. Here's my telephone number so that we can talk more about this" and the community that was fostered in and among that.[18]

This isn't merely anecdotal. Recent findings from the State of the Bible survey found that hybrid churches that offer both online and in-person services had higher percentages (46 percent) of people strongly agreeing that the church services—whether in person or online—connected them to other people.[19]

The need is for new facilitations of community in the digital age. The new community established by Christ must find a way to build a new, new community. Or at least to create new starting points for initiating and facilitating community, and those starting points must be digital. As the *New York Times* reported, "Religion has long been a fundamental way humans have formed community, and now social media companies are stepping into that role. Facebook has nearly three billion active monthly users, making it larger than Christianity worldwide, which has about 2.3 billion adherents, or Islam, which has 1.8 billion."[20] Bobby Gruenewald, creator of the popular YouVersion Bible app and a pastor at Life.Church in Oklahoma, recalled how he worked with Facebook on a Bible-verse-a-day feature in 2018 and is now working on even more collaborations. "Obviously there are different ways they ultimately, I am sure, will serve their shareholders," he said. "From our vantage point, Facebook is a platform that allows us to build community and connect with our community and accomplish our mission. So it serves I think everybody well."[21]

Will this force the rethinking of community? Undoubtedly, yes. But not all rethinking is bad.

Revisioning Community

It is grace, nothing but grace, that we are allowed to live in community.
—DIETRICH BONHOEFFER, *LIFE TOGETHER*[1]

The changes in our world are about more than just digital interactions. They are about how the digital revolution has changed what being in community even means. For example, the percentage of young people who say their favorite way to talk to friends is face to face declined from 49 percent to 32 percent in just six years. As Vicky Rideout, co-author and lead researcher of the Common Sense Media project, mused, "You can't help but say, 'Is there something big going on here?'—some fundamental shift in the way people will be communicating with each other in the future."[2] The answer, of course, is yes. A Squarespace survey found that younger generations think online presence is more important than in-person interactions. They also will look someone up online before meeting them for the first time.[3] It is simply a fact that community is being forged digitally before it is being forged physically, if it is forged physically at all.

And as we saw in the previous chapter, online community can be even more authentic than some in-person or face-to-face community younger generations have experienced. Research from Stanford University's Social Media Lab found that everyone has at least two online worlds. The "inside world" includes the people we know and who are inside our social networks. These are our family, friends, and coworkers. The second world is the stream of digital information flowing into our lives from sources we do not know personally—tweets, news articles, social-media comments—known as the "outside world." Jeff Hancock, a professor of communication and the founding director of the Stanford Social Media Lab, finds more honest communication with those close to us online: "We find that communication in the inside world tends to be more honest online, and this is in part because those messages are recorded and come from people that we will have future interactions with. We don't want a reputation as a liar, and it's easier in some ways to get caught in a lie online."[4]

The distinction between inside and outside worlds is important when evaluating online interaction. Many who dismiss that anything meaningful can occur online tend to think of outside-world engagements, not inside-world engagements. Yet it is the inside world that those who claim to experience community online are speaking of. Think of a church's strategy as connecting with someone's outside world, developing trust, and then being invited into their inside world. From there, you can extend the journey to any and all needed embodied worlds.

THE SHIFT FROM GATHERING TO CONNECTING

Because the new starting point is online, engaging people in community demands a new approach. It used to be that whatever churches did digitally was designed to serve in-person events and activities. They used the digital space to market, give information about, or offer registration for physical interactions. Going forward, the church must invert that approach and have the physical serve the digital. It is often noted that businesses must become digital organizations with physical locations. Churches too must be digital organizations with physical expressions, not physical organizations with a digital presence.

Think about companies like Sears, JCPenney, and Toys"R"Us. They emphasized big, physical footprints and in-person shopping. All three had to file for chapter 11 bankruptcy. Why? They were physical retailers that slowly adopted an online presence, behaving as if most people still wanted primarily an in-person experience. But most people didn't. They wanted to shop on Amazon, and Amazon read this perfectly. Amazon started out online, and then only later did they develop physical stores, and those were designed to enhance and serve the digital business.

The church needs to see its online presence and online community as its primary ways to initiate growth, development, discipleship, worship, ministry, and yes, embodied community—not to solely become an online entity but to shift to the physical serving the digital. We need to move away from a focus on gathering toward a focus on connecting.[5] We've bet the farm on gathering people in a building. That's a bet that won't play out in the days to come. Instead, we need to connect people in whatever way they are willing to connect. Right now and for the foreseeable future, that will be done digitally, even if it's just the starting point.

Let's stretch our thinking. Connecting digitally doesn't mean we don't gather together. Rather it means rethinking *how* we gather together and the very definition of *gathering*. It might not be physically in a building. Thousands gathered this past weekend at Meck. We talked to each other, engaged one another, experienced worship and received teaching with each other. Phone numbers and emails were exchanged. Plans were made to connect over coffee. We gave of our resources and prayed with and for one another. Pastors were pastoring, counselors were counseling. People gave their lives to Christ. All of this happened through a community gathering on an online campus. It may have been digital, but it was very real. Jesus clearly said, "For where two or three gather in my name, there am I with them" (Matt. 18:20). But he did not describe the manner of that coming together.

So what about the "one anothers" in the Bible? And there are many:

- "Be devoted to one another" (Rom. 12:10).
- "Live in harmony with one another" (Rom. 12:16).
- "Be patient, bearing with one another in love" (Eph. 4:2).
- "Spur one another on toward love and good deeds" (Heb. 10:24).
- "Accept one another" (Rom. 15:7).
- "Stop passing judgment on one another" (Rom. 14:13).
- "Be kind and compassionate to one another" (Eph. 4:32).
- "Strengthen one another" (Rom. 14:19 GNT).
- "Forgive one another" (Col. 3:13).
- "Offer hospitality to one another" (1 Peter 4:9).
- "Encourage one another" (Heb. 3:13).
- "Serve one another humbly in love" (Gal. 5:13).
- "Honor one another above yourselves" (Rom. 12:10).
- "Love one another" (John 13:34).

These exhortations might read like they can be carried out only in physical community, but is that accurate? Is the point to do these things in person, or is the point simply to see that these things are done? Isn't the real challenge the introduction of authentic community into the world of physical people, whether that world be in person or online? Stephen Lowe, the graduate chair of doctoral programs at Rawlings School of Divinity at Liberty University, puts it well:

The problem that church leaders or Christian education leaders confront today is that they're ministering in the digital age, but they're using an analog model of spiritual formation.

Their idea of community is individually oriented and place-based—there has to be a physical component, a face-to-face component, in order to be nourished. [But the] Spirit of God isn't limited to those environments.

If we really believe, as the Apostle's Creed does, in the communion of saints and this notion of the spiritual household of God that Peter talks about, . . . the household of faith that Paul talks about . . . these are concepts that embrace all realities, all experiences, whether we're talking about physical or digital.

The Holy Spirit can operate in any of those in the communion of saints in the body of Christ in the Spirit of God.

All of these function in an interactive way regardless of the environment to bring about whole person transformation into the fullness of Christ.[6]

A THIRD PLACE

So how can we begin to think more broadly about community, particularly how to introduce people to deeper levels of community through digital means and how authentic community might be served by digital means? Consider some of the apps related to community, such as Houseparty, which allows video chat with up to seven of your friends. When a couple of people open it and start chatting, a push alert that they're "in the house" is sent to everyone they're connected with. Soon, the room fills up. Such experiences have been made possible by the availability of video chat in messaging apps like Kik and Facebook Messenger, as well as standalone apps like Fam, Tribe, Airtime, ooVoo, and Houseparty. Some call it "live chilling."[7] Others are even calling it the "new third place."

There used to be only two places where you could engage community or take up social residence: in your home and in your workplace. A "third place" in the UK was the local pub. In the US, Starbucks and other coffee shops became the third place. But now, apps like Houseparty are becoming the preferred third place. Again, the pandemic accelerated the move to such apps, Houseparty included, which saw 17.2 million new downloads and 50 million sign-ups in March 2020 alone.[8] Imagine it this way: Boomers went to their friend's house after school or, as an adult, to a small group in a home. Generation X called their friends on the phone after school. Millennials used AOL Instant Messenger and later text messaging to keep up with their friends. Generation Z is back to having a house party. Only it's through their phones.

Could digital apps be a starting point for embodied community? We need to avoid two mistakes in our changing culture. One is to insist that all starting points be embodied community. The other is never to cast the vision for communal life beyond online community. Both are catastrophic. Instead, we need to keep the biblical target on the wall for authentic community but be innovative in how to step people into it.

And that will mean using social media strategically for community building.

THE ROLE OF SOCIAL MEDIA

Social media has become indispensable not only to the mission of the church but also to the building of community.

Deep Patel at *Entrepreneur* noted four social-media trends related to the building of community that are critical to understand.[9] First, more users are turning to private groups and messaging apps like Facebook Messenger, WhatsApp, and Instagram Messaging to connect with others. These messaging apps allow for the creation of more intimate groups "where we can feel secure in sharing intimate and detailed information with others." As Patel notes, this is a return to more direct communication, and it's a huge trend. A report from Pew Research found that messaging is the most popular form of digital interaction in emerging markets. So look for the continued rise of messaging apps as the connective tool of choice.[10]

Second, as people shy away from public postings and tend to connect away from public view, those trying to reach people will have to find ways to "create more private, intimate connections" without becoming overly intrusive, building "brand communities, or groups where your brand message is relevant, but where you are also receptive to direct messaging." A 2018 Facebook survey found that 69 percent of all respondents said directly messaging with a company makes them more confident in the brand. The goal is to "give audiences more meaningful connections and a feeling of being in an exclusive and intimate environment."[11]

> ## FOUR SOCIAL-MEDIA TRENDS
>
> 1. Less public, more private interactions.
> 2. Audiences want meaningful connections.
> 3. Authentic content is key to social selling.
> 4. Social media is the place to nurture trust.

Third, it's no secret that social-media users are more skeptical than ever. So when it comes to social media and shopping, they want to hear "insights from real people." User-generated content (customer reviews) are key. For a church, think testimonies. Ask people who know and love your church to write Google reviews. Encourage your members and attenders to share and invite through social media. Create stories about some of your standout volunteers.

Finally, social media is the place to nurture trust. This may be the most significant trend for churches (or at least the most important for churches to understand). Social media "isn't just a platform for marketing and advertising; it's truly the best place to nurture trust and build a relationship with [your] audience."[12] Social media offers the best opportunity to convey the value of your message or community and to engage with others on their level. Doing this will require finding ways for people "to have a free flow of dialogue and let their hair down"—not something most churches are experienced doing, much less comfortable doing.[13] But showing your "human side and increasing transparency," focusing on "fun, simple engagement," being responsive to communication, and finding meaningful ways to show "social responsibility and a deeper level of social interaction" will be key to building trust and confidence.[14] At Meck, our social-media team often poses surveys, such as what everyone's favorite drink is from our bookstore and cafe or where everyone is going on vacation. Fun reels using humor are created to highlight special events. On May 4th, "May the fourth be with you" day, we posted costumed storm troopers.

When social media is used to build rapport and trust, it can be used to invite, and few things are more effective than inviting people to experience an online campus and the community it offers.

12

Online Campus Community

We're in CA with family and friends watching
on a movie screen outside under the stars! . . .
We have all the neighbors walking over to join
us . . . we've got sixty-seven family, friends, and
neighbors all holding up phones instead of candles.
—CHRISTMAS EVE CHAT ROOM, MECK'S ONLINE CAMPUS

O ne of the ways to use social media to stair-step people toward deeper
levels of community is through digital invitations to online events.
Let's begin with something I hope is obvious: digital invites are easier to
make and respond to than physical invites. "Come to church with me this
Sunday at our campus on Browne Road" is vastly different from "Hey,
you ought to check this out online." It can be powerful when an invitation to an online community becomes a step into embodied community.

At Meck, we are finding that community-based outreach that cannot happen with an in-person service can sometimes happen through an

online campus. For example, we have groups gathering to watch in company conference rooms during lunch breaks, at breweries, and through house parties. One online attender who works at an Amazon shipping area told us in the chat room that they put the service on the sound system for their loading dock. One of my favorite stories is how a small group began attending through our online campus at their downtown office building during their Tuesday lunch hour. Word spread, and soon more and more people began attending with them—many who were not Christians. There were Hindus, Muslims, and nones. The gathering got so large that at around fifty or so people, they had to break the group up and meet in three locations. They all call Tuesday their "church day."

The organic nature of community built around an online service is compelling—not to mention the power it holds for outreach. Let me show you some chat-room comments that were gathered via screen shots from our online campus this past Christmas:

- "Our family can't be together, but we're all having watch parties from across the US! Five states for our family!"
- "This is so impressive, so funny, and not at all what I was expecting from church. (My neighbors invited us over to watch with them and I thought for sure this hour would suck.)"
- "My extended family is all here watching."
- "We haven't been to church in a long time. Thank you for this experience."
- "We're in CA with family and friends watching on a movie screen outside under the stars!" Later: "We have all the neighbors walking over to join us." Later: "We've got sixty-seven family, friends, and neighbors all holding up phones instead of candles."
- "I am tuning in with the residents of our senior center." Later: "This is just beautiful. We passed out candles to the residents."
- "Watching on break as an ER nurse; send the spirit our way!"

- "I heard about this on FB. This is awesome!"
- "My kids love MecKidz YouTube. I've learned a lot too!"
- "We've attended online for a few months and love it! We've taken classes (online) too!"

Here's a thread that captures so many of the wonderful dynamics of an online service as the front door not only into the church but into community and further engagement (names have been changed for confidentiality):

GUEST (ENTERED AS USERNAME): So is it okay to attend online or is it expected you'll come in person?

MECK MODERATOR: It is absolutely okay! You can attend online, in person, or a combination of the two! Online is how I attend church!

CRAIG AND SHARON: We have attended online for a few months and love it! We've taken classes too!

CRAIG AND SHARON: And no guilt trips or coaxing to come, Guest. Just whatever you like best.

MECK MODERATOR: Yes! Meck Online is so much more than just the service! You can attend classes, book clubs, groups, you can order from The Grounds online, and so much more!

KATHERINE: Same here, Guest. I've been attending online and have come to a few in-person events. If you live local, there's even a trail you can walk! It's a beautiful way to see the church.

MECK MODERATOR: I couldn't agree more about the trail! Grab a coffee, walk the trail, just check it out! No pressure at all.

GUEST: Thanks all. Exploring spirituality but haven't been high on church, so I appreciate the encouragement and info.

EMPATHY TECH

Another way technology not only enables community but actually enhances it is through "empathy tech," which is being introduced through virtual reality (VR). Through VR, we are able to have experiences like never before. VR evokes visceral emotional responses and allows us to see the world from a different perspective. From helping people to empathize with the refugee crisis to treating people recovering from post-traumatic stress disorder, the possibilities for the use of VR technology as it grows are endless. According to C. T. Casberg in an article titled "The Surprising Theological Possibilities of Virtual Reality," with VR "we have the opportunity to give up our own power and agency and embody the experiences of another person, to suffer with them . . . and under the right circumstances, [these experiences] can help us become more Christlike."[1]

I recall bringing the Compassion Experience, sponsored by Compassion International, to our church campus. The experience was a multitrailer production that let people walk through a poverty simulation, seeing the world those children live in, and then sponsor a child at the end. We had thousands walk through it, and hundreds of children were sponsored in the Dominican Republic, Haiti, and El Salvador. Community was built between our church and those children. When we explored doing it again, Compassion introduced us to the next level of immersion: VR headsets that would take us to where the poorest of the poor live. It was a more profound experience because in the poverty simulation, you still knew you were walking through a truck, on a movie set of sorts. But through VR, you truly felt as though you had been transported into the community where these people are living. You knew that you were really seeing someone's home, someone's neighborhood, and the conditions in which they are living. While nothing can replicate the experience of going on mission to a majority world country to see firsthand the poverty that is so pervasive there, the VR experience deepens your connection to the people you are sponsoring.

A THEOLOGY OF THE LORD'S SUPPER

As I thought through the implications of the hybrid model, nothing challenged me more than the idea of celebrating the Lord's Supper online. I hesitated to embrace the thought of any sacrament being offered online, particularly one so deeply communal as the Lord's Supper. But I knew I needed to avoid having a knee-jerk negative reaction. I had to take the digital revolution seriously and engage in robust theological reflection. So I wrestled with this question: "If someone is involved in an online campus, and the Lord's Supper is part of the service, should they be encouraged to participate in the Lord's Supper as a part of that online service?" Then I had a memory that, to me, brought great theological clarity.

When I was in seminary and was pastoring a church, one of the more meaningful ministries of the deacons was taking communion to shut-ins. (I don't know whether *shut-ins* is still the correct term, but that is what they were called back then.) As a church, we offered the Lord's Supper once a month. We always had members of the church who were physically unable to attend—they were in the hospital, in a nursing home, or in their own homes but not able to leave. So on the Sundays when we had communion, the deacons of the church fanned out across our little town after church and brought a communion kit with bread and grape juice to those people so they could also partake in the spirit of community.

The deacons would spend a few minutes talking with them, read Scripture, and pray, reminding them of the church's love and concern for them, and then share the bread and the juice with them. It was beautiful—the epitome of the church and the sacrament. Theologically, what could possibly be the problem? They were members of the church unable to physically attend, and we as the church went to them on the days we celebrated communion to include them in the spirit of community and joint celebration of the sacrament.

Fast-forward.

You're celebrating communion as a church in the 2020s, and you have people unable to attend in person who are joining you online. They may be in a hospital, in a nursing home, shut-in at home, in a hotel room as they travel on business, on vacation and watching as a family, or living in a place where they have no church home, and the online service has been their lifeline, the only church home they are able to have.

Or you're in a pandemic and everyone in your church is online.

Or you are a hybrid church that offers both online and in-person gatherings.

What do you do? Could you use the same theological and ecclesiastical reasoning that my former church applied? What if an online campus pastor said, "In just a few moments, we will be celebrating the Lord's Supper together as a family of faith. If you are a Christ follower and want to participate, go ahead now and get a piece of bread or a cracker, and some wine or juice or even water. We'll take it together in a moment as a community of faith."

Why is that different from deacons taking it to them? Today it's just the internet "taking" it to them, and they self-serve the elements. It's still done in full honor of the sacrament, under the leadership of pastors, under the authority of the church, and in the spirit of community. Diana Butler Bass, coming from the Anglican tradition, has suggested that even liturgical churches should find ways to celebrate communion online. "What I think needs to happen is that you would have a priest consecrating elements," she suggests. "The priest or minister stands there with bread and wine, does the prayers of consecration and asks the people who are streaming the service to have elements at hand—crackers and grape juice, bread and wine. What happens is that the people in the community hold up their own bread and wine while the priest is saying the prayers of consecration. The internet becomes a medium that connects the community."[2]

Are there limits to online participation in the sacraments? Our church has yet to solve whether the sacrament of baptism can be offered online or to determine whether it's even theologically solvable. Online baptism would have to maintain the public, declarative nature of the sacrament. Zoom may have possibilities, or some other future app that allows people to be physically baptized in various locations, as part of an online baptism service with each baptism made virtually public. Churches are certainly exploring this idea.[3] The point is not to move everything online. The point is to bring fresh thinking to community in the digital revolution. These three things I know: (1) we cannot bury our heads in the sand as if there are no new questions being posed to the doctrine of the church, (2) we cannot march blindly forward into the digital world as if theology doesn't matter, and (3) we cannot restrain ecclesiastical innovation as if there hasn't been a digital revolution.

SMALL IS BEAUTIFUL

E. F. Schumacher wrote a book titled *Small Is Beautiful*. You might be unfamiliar with that work, but upon its release in 1973, it became a phenomenon. Some list it among the one hundred most influential books written in modern history. It's an economics text, maybe the only one ever to reach bestseller status. The subtitle is telling: "Economics As If People Mattered." The idea is that technological development should be directed to the real needs of human beings, which means to the actual size of human beings. Human beings are small, therefore small is beautiful.[4]

Schumacher wrote in the 1970s not knowing where technology was going. He had no idea of the internet, smartphones, or artificial intelligence. But he saw that as technology progressed, it would have to be scaled to human size if human beings weren't going to be left out of the loop. Now, in some sense, that's what the smartphone did. And some of the best apps are scaled back to our size to serve us. This scaling will only become more important as "small" meets AI. For example, Siri, Echo, and other digital-assistant products bring all that technology has to offer through smartphones and the internet to bear on serving our lives.

We often talk about churches needing to get larger and smaller at the same time, meaning that as we get larger numerically, say, on weekends through in-person services, we need to get smaller by pushing assimilation and community through small groups or serving teams. But "small is beautiful" is going to bring a whole new meaning to getting larger and smaller at the same time. It will involve creatively thinking about how to bring "small" to community and how to take advantage of digital means to do so.

A CHURCH FOR
THE UNCHURCHED

The Mission

*What would be involved in a missionary
encounter between the gospel and this whole
way of perceiving, thinking, and living that
we call "modern Western culture?"*

—LESSLIE NEWBIGIN, *FOOLISHNESS TO THE GREEKS*[1]

In 2021, the Southern Baptist Convention (SBC)—the nation's largest and arguably most conservative and evangelistic Christian denomination—reported its fourteenth year of declining membership. Baptisms also declined by nearly half of the previous year's totals, marking the ninth consecutive year of decline. In 2011, SBC churches baptized 333,000; in 2020, just 123,000. Perhaps not a fair year to make a comparison, but it was just one more year of decline among many others. As Barry Hankins, historian at Baylor University, observed, "It's not hard to imagine a sense of bewilderment if not despair at the steady decline of baptisms and membership in the SBC."[2]

Southern Baptists aren't alone. A 2019 study from Exponential by Lifeway Research found that six in ten Protestant churches have plateaued or are declining in attendance, and more than half saw fewer than ten people become new Christians in the previous twelve months. Most have fewer than one hundred people attending services each week, including 21 percent who average fewer than fifty.[3] A survey of more than fifteen thousand religious congregations across the United States by Faith Communities Today (FACT) was fielded just before the pandemic. It found a median decline in attendance of 7 percent between 2015 and 2020 (fig. 13.1). It also found that half of the country's estimated 350,000 religious congregations had sixty-five or fewer people in attendance on any given weekend. In 2000, when FACT first began surveying data, the median attendance level was 137. That's a drop of more than half in just two decades.

FIGURE 13.1
Hartford Institute for Religion Research/Zondervan

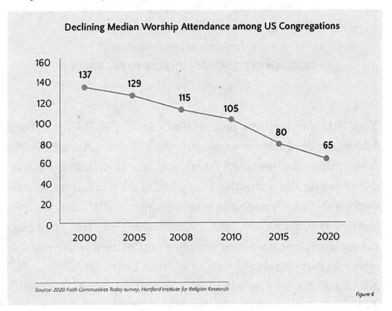

If you think these statistics are only for mainline Protestant groups, not evangelical groups, think again. Yes, mainline churches are worse off (median decline of fifty), but evangelicals have a median decline of sixty-five. The decline is across the board.

I believe we can make at least two assumptions about most Christian churches: (1) they do not want to be in decline but rather want to grow, and (2) they would like to grow as much as they can by reaching the unchurched. But the typical church isn't growing, much less reaching the unchurched. There is a massive breakdown between desire and reality. As a result, many churches are looking for something they can do. But instead they should be looking for something they can *be*. Specifically, while they are a community of faith, they should also be a church for the unchurched. Being this requires more than a new approach to evangelism; it requires becoming a true hybrid, embracing their identity as a Christian church while also embracing their mission to those who are not Christians.

THE MISSION

Being a church for the unchurched begins with a deep and abiding sense of mission. And what is that mission? It's turning irreligious people into fully devoted followers of Christ through the local church. It's the Great Commission Jesus gave to us in Matthew's gospel.

Having this mission means that when you think about the growth of the church, the outreach of the church, you are thinking about unchurched people. You are not thinking about people who are currently in other churches. You are not thinking about other churches at all. If you are a church for the unchurched, somebody else could plant a dozen new churches on your street and it wouldn't matter to you. You're after someone who isn't even interested in a church.

So what does it mean to have this kind of missional mindset? Perhaps a few examples will serve. For years, our church offered a fall festival for our community on our eighty-acre campus. It grew until it became one of the largest fall festivals in the city of Charlotte. It took enormous resources for us to offer it. Feeling uneasy about it, I gathered a team of leaders following our most recent festival and asked, "Can any of you name a single unchurched family that has come to Meck through our fall festival?" Silence. I then asked them to dig deeper into whether this event was strategic for our mission. They were to talk to other leaders and core volunteers, dig into our database, and determine whether this outreach event was reaching the unchurched. We had been so impressed by the sheer size of the event that we had simply assumed that it was. But we were not, after all, in the fall-festival business. We were in the "reaching the unchurched" business. As it turned out, despite attracting very large crowds and requiring enormous financial and volunteer investments, it was bearing little fruit.

That was the last year we had a fall festival.

Another example: during a construction phase on our campus, we were unable to use our whole auditorium while it was being expanded. We were able to scramble on most weekends, adding even more service times and days, but we couldn't handle a "big" weekend. So for our Easter service, we rented the Verizon Wireless Amphitheater (now the PNC Music Pavilion), which had a capacity of more than eighteen thousand people. Thousands of people came. We did it again the next year, even though construction on our campus had been completed. Even more attended. We added egg rolls and bounce houses. We even had bands such as NEEDTOBREATHE perform mini sets. By the fourth consecutive year, we were nearing the amphitheater's capacity. It was easily the largest single Easter service in Charlotte, perhaps the largest in the entire southeast United States.

But was it translating into growth by reaching the unchurched?

We determined that it was not. It had simply become the go-to event for Christians who wanted an Easter mega-event. But we were not in the "Easter for happily churched Christians" business, much less in the "let's grow from other churches" business. That was the last year we hosted Easter at Verizon.

SPIRITUAL NARCISSISM

There are two main ways you can grow a church. The first is through transfer growth; the second is through conversion growth. Transfer growth is growing through subtraction—subtracting people from other churches. Conversion growth is growth through addition—adding people who were never before part of a church. Despite the rhetoric and mission statements, impassioned sermons and vision casting, the overwhelming majority of churches are focused almost exclusively on transfer growth. Their outreach is *for* Christians and *to* Christians. Their weekend services are designed solely with Christians in mind. Their website is designed to speak to and serve not simply Christians but their attenders and members. Everything about the church's public posture is clear: we're for and about us.

You ask, "Well, isn't that what a Christian church is supposed to be?" No, it's not. Not when it comes to our mission. Many want to make the mission about the already convinced instead of those who are far from God. Some are even outspoken about focusing solely on the needs of believers as the way to be evangelistic. Tell me if this sounds familiar: "There is no real need to focus on evangelism or outreach. It's not healthy. The focus needs to be on feeding the already convinced and, from that feeding, evangelism will naturally take place. The most important thing for a church to do is to focus on the already convinced, and then the already convinced will naturally turn outward and reach out to friends and family members with the message of the gospel. The role of the church is for the care and feeding of Christians. If you target non-Christians for outreach, you will diminish your responsibility to serve Christians."

It's a very appealing message to the average Christian. The focus remains firmly on them and their felt needs. They can be fed but not feed, be served but not serve, embrace the rhetoric of evangelism without its practice or its sacrifice. It's no wonder it's where most churches have landed. So how is that working for us? Not very well.

The deeper issue that I have attempted to lay bare for much of my vocational life is spiritual narcissism. Spiritual narcissism has invaded the Christian community. Eavesdrop, for a moment, on how some Christians talk or the kinds of things they post: "I want to go where I'm fed," not where I can learn to feed myself, much less feed others. "I need to be ministered to," as if ministry in the life of the Christ follower is something that happens *to* me instead of something I make happen for others. We walk out of a worship service and say, "I didn't get anything out of it," as if the purpose of worship is what I get out of it instead of what God gets out of it. We engage with an experience and say, "That wasn't very moving," instead of pondering whether God was moved by the engagement.

Where did this self-absorbed spiritual mindset come from? It wasn't from our leader. He didn't talk that way. Instead, Jesus said, "For even the Son of Man did not come to be served, but to serve, and to give his life as a ransom for many" (Mark 10:45); "whoever wants to become great among you must be your servant, and whoever wants to be first must be your slave" (Matt. 20:26–27); "yet not my will, but yours be done" (Luke 22:42). Yet spiritual narcissism has invaded our thinking, where the individual needs and desires of the believer are the center of attention. As a result, the church has lost its missional energy and focus.

Discipleship and evangelism are not mutually exclusive. But so much Christian discipleship and spiritual formation is narcissistic. It's all about the felt spiritual needs of the Christian. There is little in the way of discipling for the mission itself. Authentic discipleship, if it should result in anything, should result in a missional life like the life of

Jesus, who came, he said, to seek and to save the lost. It should result in a community of faith asking, even begging, "How can we die to ourselves, like Jesus did, to reach a lost and dying world?"

WHATEVER HAPPENED TO EVANGELISM?

But there is little in the way of that kind of discipleship. A survey of churches in Canada found that 65 percent of church leaders say evangelism hasn't been a priority for their congregations over the last several years. Only 9 percent said it was a high priority for members of their congregation to share their faith. These were not mainline churches. The majority of those surveyed came from evangelical traditions, including leaders from Baptist churches, Pentecostal churches, the Christian and Missionary Alliance, the Evangelical Free Church, the Church of the Nazarene, the Foursquare Church, and the Salvation Army.[4]

There is a lack of discipleship not only on the importance of evangelism but also on its theological necessity. A survey of self-identifying born-again Christians between the ages of eighteen and thirty-nine found that nearly 70 percent do not believe that Jesus is the only way to God. They were asked whether they disagree with the following statement: "Muhammad, Buddha, and Jesus all taught valid ways to God." Most born-again Christians said, "No, I do not disagree."[5]

> A SURVEY OF CHURCHES IN CANADA FOUND THAT 65 PERCENT OF CHURCH LEADERS SAY THAT EVANGELISM HASN'T BEEN A PRIORITY FOR THEIR CONGREGATIONS OVER THE LAST SEVERAL YEARS. ONLY 9 PERCENT SAID IT WAS A HIGH PRIORITY FOR MEMBERS OF THEIR CONGREGATION TO SHARE THEIR FAITH.

But even when evangelism is highlighted and a robust theology of the exclusive nature of salvation in relation to Jesus is present, there is still a missing ingredient: relationships with lost people. A report from the Pew Research Center found that Americans have become less likely to even know an evangelical Christian.[6] Yet if our mission is the evangelization and transformation of our world through the local church, then there is one thing that should go without saying: we should be engaging that world.

So why aren't we? One reason is we are submerged in a Christian subculture where the only time we break free from our small-group Bible studies, Christian fitness groups, and church gatherings is to venture out to Chick-fil-A. Another darker reason is raw animus. We look at people outside of the faith as the enemy. It's us versus them, black hats versus white hats, good guys versus bad guys. We line up as the pro-family, Christian-radio-listening, homeschooling types against the NPR-listening, gay-marriage-supporting *Game of Thrones* watchers. Yet the fact remains that the way someone far from God draws close to him is if someone close to God goes far to reach them (Rom. 10:14–15).

To be a church for the unchurched requires a clear and compelling sense of mission. Having that sense of mission will result in selflessness and a commitment to evangelistic relationships with people who are far from God. That is what a church should *be*.

Now for what a church for the unchurched can *do*.

YOUR CHURCH MUSE

Reaching a post-Christian world demands contextualizing the message of the gospel—not, as we saw in chapter 6, changing it in substance but recasting it. The goal is translation, not transformation. But still very much translation. As Lesslie Newbigin has written,

The gospel is addressed to human beings, to their minds and hearts and consciences, and calls for their response. Human beings only exist as members of communities which share a common language, customs, ways of ordering economic and social life, ways of understanding and coping with their world. If the gospel is to be understood, if it is to be received as something which communicates truth about the real human situation, if it is, as we say, to "make sense," it has to be communicated in the language of those to whom it is addressed and has to be clothed in symbols which are meaningful to them. . . . It must, as we say, "come alive." Those to whom it is addressed must be able to say, "Yes, I see. This is true for me, for my situation."[7]

So who is your church muse?

When Anheuser Busch InBev wanted to deliver a global brand strategy for Budweiser that could be activated in a local fashion, they decided to create an aspirational Bud "Muse." They personified a composite of their customers so that they could ask themselves at every marketing juncture, "What would Will do?"[8]

This is an important step for a church to take. Wherever you live, you can create a muse for who you are trying to reach. For many reasons, the muse for our church is a young, unchurched, married, professional male. Our muse does not function to exclude people from any age, sex, or background. Obviously, all are welcomed and celebrated. But for our area, this is the typical unchurched person we are attempting to reach. When it comes to outreach, this is who we have in mind. When it comes to opening our front door, designing our website, crafting a digital ad, or even how we position ourselves physically through buildings or grounds, it is with this person in mind.

Many churches will want to resist focusing on a single type of person in the name of wanting to reach everyone. But if you think you're reaching everyone, in reality you're reaching no one. You simply can't craft an effective penetration without a target. The mission we have been given is specific: it's for the person who is not yet in a relationship with Jesus. Once you have that mission clearly in mind, you can take the next strategic step and begin reaching out to them where they are, which means online.

Reaching Out Online

"Everyone who calls on the name of the LORD will be saved." But how can they call on him to save them unless they believe in him? And how can they believe in him if they have never heard about him? And how can they hear about him unless someone tells them?

—APOSTLE PAUL (ROM. 10:13–15 NLT)

According to the World Economic Forum, research to determine what to buy or what to do has become the dominant reason for using social media. The number of people who say they use social media because a lot of their friends use it has declined (–16 percent); so has the number who use it to stay in touch with their friends (–9 percent). Reasons for using social media that are on the rise: to network for work (+9 percent), to follow celebrities and celebrity news (+27 percent), and to research and find products to buy (+30 percent). That last bit of information should stand out to church leaders. People are obviously going online to explore and research, but increasingly they are doing so through social media. As we saw earlier, the study found that 64 percent of Generation Z and 62 percent of millennials use social channels for product research or state that social channels are influential in choosing products.[1]

Most churches make one of two mistakes when it comes to marketing. Either they fail to market their church or message in any way, or they market it ineffectively. During my church planting days, the internet was a nonfactor. You would put ads in the newspaper, make flyers, or, if you were cutting-edge, use direct mail. Unfortunately, many churches, if they make any marketing effort at all, are still using those approaches. But with the vast majority of the unchurched community reachable almost exclusively online, we need to rethink marketing our churches.

Which brings us to digital marketing.

Philip Kotler, known as the father of modern marketing, has argued for a revolution in his discipline that he calls Marketing 4.0. The first major marketing shift was from product-driven marketing (1.0) to customer-centric marketing (2.0), and from that to human-centric marketing (3.0). The idea of Marketing 3.0 was to create products, services, and company cultures that embraced and reflected human values. But the digital revolution calls for an entirely new approach that divides all traditional marketing that has gone on before from the digital marketing that now must be the focus of our efforts.[2]

Just as the front door of the church has gone digital, so has outreach. While it is easy to have a negative reaction to Instagrammable Bibles, TikTok preachers, or celebrity-fueled "cool" churches, "there is without a doubt a change underway," notes an article on *YPulse*, "a shift in how religious organizations and individuals are attempting to win over the next generations. And by being a more constant presence in the space where young people are spending their time (social platforms) these efforts could earn followings—even if they're just on feeds, and not in pews."[3]

There are three online outreach headlines: First, your website is still central. Apps serve people digitally, but they are not the way people explore your church. So you must make your website the anchor of your outreach. Second, people will make their digital decision about your church in seconds. This means you must engage them as quickly as possible. Third, the goal is a click, not a visit. The visit—whether in person or online—follows the click. Or as I have heard quipped, "Bricks follow clicks." The target on the wall is to get them to check you out online, most commonly through your website or online campus.

This last statement is worth explaining a bit. You are not trying to use digital marketing to achieve a physical visit. That may sound counterintuitive, but think of it as stair-stepping someone into a particular action. In various speaking events, I have often demonstrated this idea to people by walking over to a table and asking, "How many of you can do a standing jump and land on top of this?" Few can. But then I bring a chair over to the table and ask, "How many of you could first step onto this chair and then, from the chair, step onto the table?" Almost everyone can do that. Then I make the simple point that when we ask an unchurched person to attend in person as their first step to getting to know us, we are asking them to do a standing jump onto the table. The online invitation should first be to a chair.

So how do you do that?

There is still a place for traditional marketing (for example, mailers to the physical addresses of new residents), but the real penetration will be from digital marketing.

> ### THREE ONLINE OUTREACH HEADLINES
>
> 1. Your website is still central.
> 2. Digital decisions about your church will be made in seconds.
> 3. The goal is a click, not a visit.

As our church's marketing director likes to put it, we are meeting our consumers right where they are: online. We are using a mix of mediums that work together to maximize impressions. This involves running a *paid search* campaign on not only Google but all search engines so that when anyone, anywhere is searching for us directly, looking for a church, or searching any of the keywords we are using, we will show up at the top of the search page. We run a *retargeting display* campaign so that anyone who has searched for us or landed on our website will be served future ads as a result of their initial interest.

With traditional radio in decline, we focus on *digital radio* ads with a mix on Pandora, Spotify, iHeart Radio, and Sirius XM that can be much more targeted than on traditional radio. After doing our research and finding that our target demographic spends most of their time with *digital video*, specifically YouTube, we invest a good amount of outreach effort in that medium. We also run a *pre-roll campaign* with a focus on YouTube to be sure we are in front of the people whose attention we are trying to capture. We do an *email marketing* campaign a handful of times a year that is sent to everyone who has given us permission to contact them throughout the years, using our own database. We do not purchase email lists, so we know that each person receiving the email communication has some sort of interest in or experience with Meck. Finally, we run a *social-media campaign* (which is different from simply boosting a post), primarily on Facebook and Instagram, where we have run tests to determine where we have been able to gain the most traction. With all of these mediums, and with cross-device technology, we are able to be in front of more people, more times, on more devices. And again, all of these efforts are produced with an unchurched person in mind.

If all of this sounds "big church," think again. Financially, digital marketing is vastly cheaper than more traditional forms of marketing, whether it's newspaper ads or direct mail. Further, most sites such as Google have online tutorials and easy step-by-step guidelines for getting started. The nomenclature may be intimidating, but the actual practice of marketing digitally is not.

Many of these marketing efforts are less expensive than you might think, but more important, they are good and effective investments: more than one out of every four unchurched people responds positively to a video about a church posted on a church website, sent via email, or posted on social media. As many as 18 percent are receptive to an advertisement on Facebook.[4]

One of the newer approaches to reaching people outside of the church through digital marketing is the use of "big data." Companies such as Gloo mine online data to assist churches' outreach efforts. Analyzing personal data and online activities can help churches reach out to people who are most likely to be open to their message. As an article in the *Wall Street Journal* describes it, "Just as retailers or political candidates send out online ads to groups of people with particular characteristics—including demographics, browsing activity, purchasing behavior and other factors that advertising platforms allow clients to choose—churches can use Gloo to show ads to groups of people they believe are most receptive to becoming members, or they think they could help."[5]

ONLINE OUTREACH

1. Paid Search
2. Retargeting Display
3. Digital Radio
4. Digital Video
5. Pre-Roll
6. Email Marketing
7. Social Media

Westside Family Church, a nondenominational Christian church near Kansas City, has used Gloo to try to reach people who are dealing with financial problems, as well as those struggling in the pandemic, through online ads. "The church is committed to going out at whatever cost to find that one lost sheep that needs help," said Randy Frazee, lead pastor of Westside. "There are a lot of people who are in pain and isolated," Frazee said. "If you don't come to church, the church will come to you."[6]

ENGAGING ONLINE ATTENDERS

So what do you do once you have an online attender? How do you keep them engaged beyond continuing to offer online services?

One of the simplest approaches, though it does take some work to set up, is what is often called a "drip campaign." The idea is to automate a series of contacts with someone via text and email on next steps they can take. The more information you have about them, the more personalized this can be. But the idea is to connect with them in some way every few weeks, encouraging them to attend an online class, continue their attendance through the online campus, volunteer for a serving day, or explore a series of YouTube videos that answer questions about the Christian faith. You may run several different "drips" according to how you group people. In the most sophisticated of systems, drips can be parsed out based on information such as sex, age, marital status, the presence or absence of children, or spiritual background.

Digital outreach isn't just connecting with people online when they are online but continuing to reach out to them digitally as part of any and all in-person engagement. Much has been written since the 1980s about how to open the physical front door, from casual dress and contemporary music to children's ministry and intentional guest services. I won't rehash such things here because they have been well cared for in other places, including my own writings.[7] What hasn't been written about is the need to open the front door "phygitally."

THE FOURTH INDUSTRIAL REVOLUTION

The word *phygital* comes from the combination of *physical* and *digital*, and it is applied to spaces where the two come together seamlessly. It might not sound like much, but to many people's thinking, it is at the heart of a fourth industrial revolution.

In chapter 4, we discussed the first three industrial revolutions that have transpired. The fourth industrial revolution, first identified by Klaus Schwab, founder and executive chairman of the Geneva-based World Economic Forum (WEF), "refers to how a combination of technologies are changing the way we live, work and interact." According to an article by Elizabeth Shulze, Schwab argues that "a technological revolution is underway 'that is blurring the lines between the physical, digital and biological spheres.'" The fourth industrial revolution, she writes, "refers to how technologies like artificial intelligence, autonomous vehicles and the internet of things are merging with human's physical lives. Think of voice-activated assistants, facial ID recognition or digital health-care sensors." According to Schwab, "These technological changes are drastically altering how individuals, companies and governments operate, ultimately leading to a societal transformation similar to previous industrial revolutions." Zvika Krieger, the head of technology policy and partnerships at WEF, notes that what sets the fourth industrial revolution apart from its predecessor is twofold: "the gap between the digital, physical and biological worlds is shrinking, and technology is changing faster than ever."[8]

The idea of the phygital grew out of the need for a seamless flow between the physical and the digital. As Eben Esterhuizen put it in an article on *Bizcommunity*, in relation to the retail world, "Innovative phygital business models, where bricks and mortar and digital seamlessly integrate, are popping up across the globe. But the best phygital experiences still remain aligned with old-school sales strategies: customer attraction, retention, engagement, experiences, loyalty and the brand itself. The factors that keep shifting are shopping behaviour and new technology. The upshot is: to keep in the retail game, phygital is the way to go and it's currently an adapt or die situation."[9]

THE PHYGITAL EXPERIENCE

So what is a phygital experience like? It's ordering your groceries online and picking them up in person. It's touchless pay when you fill up your car with gas. It's scanning a QR code at a restaurant to look at the menu.

It's checking in for a flight using a kiosk, then approaching the desk to check your bags. As an article on *Mobiquity* put it, "Phygital is about bridging the relationship between a user (human) and activity (company) and making that experience so effortless that your customers don't even notice that their life has become easier."[10]

First, think about people's phygital desires, particularly among the younger generations. According to PYMTS.com, "These connected souls value the experience of being connected. . . . And when they shop, they are looking for an experience in-store that is like, or connected outright to, the world they know online." Ninety-eight percent of Generation Z shop in physical stores, searching "beyond the 'buy button'" for an experience that takes place in multiple dimensions.[11] This is why the latest entries into brick-and-mortar retail are, ironically, such companies as Amazon and Google. Even Apple is hard at work with a new set of retail stores that are designed almost entirely for experience. Their goal? Change "Meet me at Starbucks" to "Meet me at Apple."[12]

Or think about retail banking, which has experienced a steep decline in branch visits because of the move to online banking. In 2017 alone, 1,700 branches closed. So what does the banking future hold? Analysts are pointing to at least four powerful paths to connect with customers:[13]

1. **ONLINE AND MOBILE** for secure electronic transfers on all tech platforms and for nearly all transaction types, including payments and trading.
2. **TELEPHONIC SERVICES** for information, problem-solving, and help.
3. **ENHANCED ATMS** with private, secure enclosures for large cash deposits, cashier's checks, money orders, bonds, and/or video chats.
4. **A REDEFINED IN-BRANCH EXPERIENCE** that accounts for the other connections.

What's key to understanding the phygital experience is that last banking dynamic: a redefined in-branch experience that accounts for the other connections. Here's how it is described in an article posted on *FinTech*:

> This demographic demands experiences which are fast-moving, yet at the same time they are keen to ensure that the product or service they are interested in is suitable for them, usually by visiting a store and experiencing it "in the flesh." A Barclays report exploring the customer trends of Gen Z found that 46 percent of those surveyed would visit a brick-and-mortar store to find out more about a product or service before committing to purchase it. These findings suggest that both physical and digital elements of the customer journey should work together to allow customers to view and discuss products and services in the physical environment, yet purchase said product/service digitally at a later date, if incumbent banks want to continue to remain relevant among younger users.[14]

Going phygital is not limited to the banking industry but is sweeping every aspect of retail. For example, "A furniture retailer could try to bridge its online and real-world sales strategies with an app that allows a potential buyer to see how a couch on display in a showroom might look in their living room."[15] Let's stick with shopping and think through further the potential phygital dynamic. If someone has a product in their shopping cart while shopping online, it's seamlessly integrated into their in-store shopping experience. The more common in-store phygital tech includes self-scanning, digital signage tablets, and smart tags. Other innovations being tested are AR-powered virtual demos, smart mirror beacons, personal in-store digital avatars, face-detection software that can guess a shoppers' gender and age, as well as interactive fitting rooms with a touch-screen kiosk. All the while keeping the human connection.[16]

So going phygital does not mean eliminating bricks and mortar but rather recognizing the importance of integrating what we do physically with what we do digitally, and, ideally, creating a synergy between the two that is more strategic than either way alone. Whatever its manifestation, becoming phygital is not a choice but a necessity. As David Stubbs at J. P. Morgan Private Bank wrote in an email to MSNBC, "Technology, and specifically digital technology, is so intertwined with many businesses, as well as our social and economic lives, that trying to separate 'tech' from 'non-tech' is becoming increasingly redundant."[17]

THE PHYGITAL CHURCH

Writing about her experience attending Life.Church, Corrina Laughlin, though she does not use the word *phygital*, describes how a church can be phygital.

> Although some people brought their own physical Bible, most, like me, used the Life.Church YouVersion Bible App during the service.... On the YouVersion App you can search sermon plans, and I found the plan for the day I was visiting, and I followed along and took notes on my iPhone. The app ... [offers] "badges" to users when they perform certain functions on the app. For example, I earned a "YouVersion Badge" when I subscribed to a reading plan on the app. The app also integrated with iOS functionalities. Because I have installed YouVersion on my iPhone, when I send a text message, my phone offers a widget that would allow me to send Bible verse from the app through text.... And in this way, Life.Church's app folds into the digital habitus of its users.[18]

At Meck, our app also seamlessly integrates with physical events and services. You can use it to check your children in to our children's ministry, order a beverage from our coffee shop, listen to a weekend message, register for a class, find out the name of a song that was used in worship and download it, and order a book from our bookstore. Even before you leave the building, you can post a prayer request, send a question for a pastor, send out an e-vite to friends to join you next week or to check out the service online, or explore suggested next steps from that weekend's message, including recommended reading.

But what makes an in-person event at a building phygital isn't simply an app. Throughout our building are QR codes, either on signs or screens, that can be scanned for more information on a given ministry or event. Guests may even get a push notification related to their experience, such as a next step, as they are leaving.

As you can see, much of the promise that going phygital holds depends not simply on people having smartphones but on your church having an app. You might think your church is too small to have its own app or that having one would be too expensive. But you would be surprised at how inexpensive a basic, custom-designed app for your church actually is. And it's worth the investment. It's simply a fact that of all the changes that have occurred in recent years, the one that is widely seen as remaining firmly in place is the preference for remote interactions.[19] One of the more obvious reasons is convenience. And almost everyone has a smartphone. According to the latest findings by the Pew Research Center, the percentage of Americans who own a smartphone jumped from 35 percent in 2011 to 97 percent in 2021.[20] And we like using them. On average, people check their phones ninety-six times each day. That's once every ten minutes. Texting is now so common among all age groups that even baby boomers (the oldest of whom are now seventy-five years old) are "seven times more likely to text than talk in-person and twice as likely to send a text rather than dial a phone number." And no one over the age of seventy would ever be called a digital native.[21]

And what are we doing on our phones? According to app analytics company App Annie's "State of Mobile 2022" report, people in the world's top ten mobile markets for Android spent a solid 4.8 hours browsing apps each day. As an article on *Mashable* commented on the findings, "That's roughly a third of our waking hours." And seven out of every ten of those minutes were spent on "social, photo, and video apps."[22]

Beyond going phygital, the power and purpose of a church app is that it keeps the church together for more than an hour or two on Sunday. You go with people by going with their phone, and people are very much doing life on and through their phone. An app lets you meet them there. An app is particularly critical to reaching and serving younger generations. For Generation Z, an app is more important than a website. They do everything through their phones and other mobile devices.

> ACCORDING TO THE LATEST FINDINGS BY THE PEW RESEARCH CENTER, THE PERCENTAGE OF AMERICANS WHO OWN A SMARTPHONE JUMPED FROM 35 PERCENT IN 2011 TO 97 PERCENT IN 2021.

The purpose of any app is to serve and increase any and all engagement. And a good app does. According to Subsplash's Church App landing page, when a church adds an app, they can expect to see at least three times as many people use their app as attend on Sunday, a 50 percent increase in the number of sermon plays, and a 10 percent or more increase in monthly giving.[23] Think about the YouVersion Bible App, which in 2021 hit half a billion downloads.[24] YouVersion founder Bobby Gruenwald recounts the moment the idea came to him while waiting in line at an airport: "I had struggled to consistently read the Bible, even though I desired to—I wanted to. I just couldn't quite find the interface with it that fit with kind of the busyness and the travel and the way that my life was at the time. So there in the airport that day, this idea came for YouVersion."[25]

The app now offers 2,600 versions of the Bible in more than 1,760 languages and provides guided reading plans, devotionals, podcast recommendations, video teaching resources, and features that encourage consistency and community engagement when reading the Bible. "It started as a question," notes YouVersion's blog. "What if we could use technology to help people engage more consistently with the Bible? . . . Every time someone installs YouVersion, they're getting instant access to a Community centered around the Bible. A Community that's inviting God to shape their lives through Scripture, Bible Plans, and Prayer."[26]

That's the vision of any church app.

There will be some who decry reading the Bible on an app, as if something will somehow be lost through the medium. But a Bible app might very well be the only way younger people will ever even consider digesting the Scriptures. While only 7 percent of Elders prefer reading the Bible on a screen such as a phone or a tablet, the younger the generation, the more that percentage increases: 16 percent of baby boomers, 30 percent of Gen Xers, 36 percent of millennials, and 38 percent of Gen Zers.[27]

During a recent series of Christmas services, one of our backstage volunteers was a young teenager who, when not performing one of her duties, was glued to her phone. Not in the normal way you see people glued to their phone—the scrolling was less frenetic and there was no texting. She was just really into what she was viewing. She seemed to be reading something long-form. After seeing her do this several times over the course of multiple services, I asked her what she was engaging. She

> WHEN A CHURCH ADDS AN APP, THEY CAN EXPECT TO SEE AT LEAST THREE TIMES AS MANY PEOPLE USE THEIR APP AS ATTEND ON SUNDAY, A 50 PERCENT INCREASE IN THE NUMBER OF SERMON PLAYS, AND A 10 PERCENT OR MORE INCREASE IN MONTHLY GIVING.

looked up and said, "I want to read through the entire Bible, and while I'm on break, I wanted to get through as much of it as I could." We can talk about whether it's best to read the Bible on paper or on a screen, but as a pastor, I am just delighted people are reading it.

Process and Event

"Would you tell me, please, which way I ought to walk from here?"

"That depends a good deal on where you want to get to," said the Cat.

"I don't much care where—" said Alice.

"Then it doesn't matter which way you walk," said the Cat.

—LEWIS CARROLL, *ALICE'S ADVENTURES IN WONDERLAND*[1]

I usually have several movies or series on my list to watch on various streaming services. I'm much more discriminating when it comes to venturing to an actual theater. That list is shorter because it has a higher price tag. A movie that I certainly did not have on either list (though I liked many of the actors) was a 2017 movie titled *The Greatest Showman*. I'm not sure why. Maybe it was because *The Last Jedi* had come out around the same time, and I'm not so much a "go to a new movie every week" kind of person as a "wait for it to come out on Netflix" kind. Or maybe it was because it didn't hook me. Yes, P. T. Barnum is a fascinating historical figure, but it didn't seem like a movie that was going to really detail his life. And while I really like Hugh Jackman, this wasn't exactly *Wolverine*.

Then I got a text from my youngest daughter. She *raved* about the movie, so much so that when she came into town on her birthday, she wanted to see it again with her brothers. Then *they* raved about it. So I had a young mom with three kids loving it as well as two "guy's guys" who would pass on the Hallmark Channel for a rerun of *Braveheart* any day of the week. Then I overheard more than a few people on our church staff say, "Have you seen this movie? It's great! You should see it! Don't pay attention to the reviews, or to what it's about—it's just so good." This led my wife to ask me if I wanted to go, and by that time, I was ready.

It's one of my favorite movies of all time.

Why did I go see it? Word of mouth. The recommendations of others moved me from almost a complete lack of interest, to going and becoming a raving fan. And it wasn't just any word of mouth; it was the word of mouth of those I like, know, and trust: family, friends, people I work with, people who live nearby. And because word of mouth came from so many people, I saw the film.

Word of mouth is the church's secret power to penetrate the world. It always has been. Michael Green wrote a treatise on the explosive growth of the early Christian church in the first century. Let me save you a few hundred pages of reading. His conclusion can be summarized in a single sentence: they shared the gospel like it was gossip over the backyard fence.[2]

During more than three decades of outreach at Meck, we've tracked why first-time guests come to our church. Every first-time guest who lets us know they attended is asked four questions in a follow-up survey:

1. What did you notice first?
2. What did you like best?
3. How could we have improved?
4. How did you hear about the church?

The number one reason people come to our church has never changed, and there's never been a close second. The most cited reason for attending has always been "Invited by a friend." And it is that culture of invitation that permeates a church for the unchurched. Research coming out of the Billy Graham Center Institute at Wheaton College found that 79 percent of unchurched people are fine with Christians talking about their faith if those Christians value it,[3] and half would respond positively to an invitation to attend a church if the invitation came from a friend.[4] Another reason a culture of invitation will continue to be decisive, even in our day of social media, is that social media is trending toward becoming more private. As we saw in chapter 11, younger users in particular are much more private and share personal information only in friend groups.[5] So social media likely one day won't have the outreach potential it has now.

Once a friend who has been invited becomes engaged with the church, they've embarked on a process of evangelism that in a post-Christian culture takes on new life.

THE IMPORTANCE OF PROCESS, NOT JUST EVENT

In earlier eras, evangelism was almost entirely treated as an event. You presented the gospel and called for a decision. That's all there was to evangelism. That was the era of Sunday school and door-to-door visitation, busing and revivals. All were largely event-oriented approaches, giving a cold-call presentation and asking for an immediate decision.

It often worked.

But as our culture became post-Christian and lacked spiritual literacy, evangelism became both process and event. Now it's necessary to invest in and facilitate someone's journey down the line of faith (the process of evangelism) to that point where they have gained enough answers to consider an invitation to respond (the event of evangelism).

Think of it this way. According to a 2017 *Wall Street Journal* article,

> The Scotts Miracle-Gro Co. has started offering gardening lessons for young homeowners that cover basic tips—really, really basic—like making sure sunlight can reach plants. Jim King, senior vice president of corporate affairs for Scotts, said: "These are simple things we wouldn't have really thought to do or needed to do fifteen to twenty years ago. But this is a group who may not have grown up putting their hands in the dirt growing their vegetable garden in Mom and Dad's back yard." So companies such as Scotts, Home Depot Inc., Proctor and Gamble Co., Williams-Sonoma Inc's West Elm and the Sherwin-Williams Co. are hosting classes and online tutorials to teach such basic skills as how to mow the lawn, use a tape measure, mop a floor, hammer a nail and pick a paint color.[6]

People need to be educated before they can even begin to consider a purchasing decision. Or even a purchasing *need*.

It is no different with faith. Think of a scale from one to ten, with one representing someone as far away from God as possible and ten representing the moment when they come to saving knowledge and faith. We used to have a culture where people were at eight on the scale.

People at eight on the scale brought so much to the evangelism table: a belief in truth, a belief that God exists, a Judeo-Christian values system, a sense of guilt when they violated that system, a positive church background, and a respect for church leaders. When people are at eight, an event-oriented approach can push them to ten.

But most people in our culture are not at eight. At best, they're at three.

That means we need to move them from three to eight, where they can begin to responsibly engage the call to decide.

But what are we trying to accomplish in that process? What do we need to do to move them down the line? It used to be that the typical unchurched person who engaged our church considered themselves to be a Christian. Often they were not. They were cultural Christians at best. And so the evangelistic process was as follows: (1) they came thinking they were Christians; (2) they discovered that they actually were not when they learned what crossing the line of faith means, what the life of faith line entails, and had common objections against Christianity addressed and the faith explained to them; and (3) they accepted the invitation to cross the line of faith when they were ready. They came thinking they were Christians, they found out they weren't, and then we helped them cross the line.

Here's the new evangelistic process: (1) they come thinking they have rejected Christianity; (2) they learn that they really haven't, because they have an inaccurate idea of the Christian faith; and (3) we introduce them to the real thing and invite them when they are ready to cross the line of faith. They come thinking they are not Christians, we tell them we reject what they reject too, and then we cast the vision of a life in Christ.

You can see that while these processes have different starting points, they are built around the same two dynamics: explanation and incarnation. The explanation of authentic faith and the collective incarnation of authentic faith—in a way that is both winsome and compelling—propels people down the line. This simple idea that evangelism is both process and event is critical to reaching a post-Christian world. We used to have language of "leading someone to faith," which always meant leading someone in the sinner's prayer. Now leading someone to faith is leading them down a line to the point where they can contemplate praying the prayer.

Understanding this dynamic perfectly, Carey Nieuwhof outlines the five ways evangelism in a post-Christian world has become process oriented:

1. Embracing the question is as important as giving an answer.
2. Steering the conversation is better than pushing for a conclusion.

3. Being open is more effective than being certain.
4. Arrogance, smugness, and superiority are dead.
5. The timeline is longer.[7]

By *embracing the question*, Nieuwhof says, you are embracing the process. He gives the example of someone asking about reincarnation. Rather than responding dismissively, "Well, Christians don't believe in that," a better response would be, "That's a great question. We're actually more into resurrection. Would you like to hear about that?" *Steering a conversation* is all about listening, refusing to judge, affirming the intent of questions, and steering the conversation back to truth. *Being open*, similarly, is seeking to understand where people are coming from, listening deeply, and affirming when you can your own similar doubts and questions. *Avoiding arrogance, smugness, and superiority* is self-evident. And finally Nieuwhof joins me on process-event issues by noting that the *time is longer*. He's right that "people who come to faith when pressured often leave it after a few years. . . . Conversely, the people who come to faith on their own timeline tend to be flourishing years down the road."[8]

TWO TYPES OF CHURCHES AND THE NEED FOR A THIRD

Related to evangelism as both process and event is how the Christian faith is explained and presented along the way.

Let me oversimplify and say that there are two main types of churches that say they want to reach the unchurched but have different approaches to moving people from three to eight. The first believes it is vital to proclaim the truth of the Christian message to a darkened world. Sin must be named, behavior must be called out, and falsehoods demolished. The difference between the church and the world, the message of the gospel and dominant cultural values, must be clearly delineated. People will not come to faith unless called to repentance, and that means convincing them of their sin and then convicting them of their sin.

The second type of church believes it is vital to identify with the world—if not embrace and reflect it—in every way possible to build relational bridges and find cultural acceptance. The goal is not to call people out but to welcome them in. That means burying those aspects of the Christian faith that are culturally offensive. The goal is "Jesus as friend," "Jesus as mentor," "Jesus as accepter."

These descriptions are, of course, caricatures. But they reveal a fundamental choice in the swing of an important pendulum. The first type of church is concerned to stake out the teaching of the Christian faith in all of its countercultural glory. The second is concerned with being accepted by culture so that people in that culture feel accepted. The first type of church swings heavily toward truth, the second type of church swings heavily toward grace.

Neither swing is a good one, at least when it comes to reaching the unchurched. In his day, Jesus was attractive to people who were considered sinners and spiritual outcasts. They flocked to hear him teach, they invited him to their weddings, and they introduced him to their friends at parties. All this while Jesus spoke openly about sin and repentance and the need for a transformed life. How could this be? It was the result, as John points out in the opening chapter of his gospel, of Jesus' coming "full of grace and truth" (John 1:14).

It's the *and* in that sentence that matters.

Grace without truth is what Dietrich Bonhoeffer famously called "cheap."[9] It is sentimentality at best, licentiousness at worst. Unless grace is accompanied by the truth about death-inducing sin, nothing makes it "amazing." Grace has its fullest meaning and holds its greatest power when it is applied to the fatal nature of sin made clear through the proclamation of truth.

Yet truth without grace is also wanting. Truth without grace leaves us in the arid, brutal wasteland of legalism and judgmentalism. Orthodoxy may be upheld, sin may be condemned, the culture wars may be engaged, but spiritual pride runs rampant and little is irenic or arresting. Unchurched people see the stones in our hands, ready to be thrown at a moment's notice.

What we need is the inviting and electric dynamic of bearing both truth and grace that the people who encountered Jesus experienced. For example, think of the Samaritan woman at the well, who, at the end of a candid conversation with Jesus about her serial promiscuity, felt like everyone else should have a revealing chat with him too. "Come!" she said to everyone she could find in her town. "See a man who told me everything I ever did" (John 4:29). Jesus brought truth to bear on her life, but it led not to a relational breakdown but to relational attraction. How could this be? Only because with the truth came grace—an acceptance for her as a person who mattered to God. Somehow, some way, Jesus made her realize that she was both broken and beloved, in need of saving but cherished beyond worth.

Truth without grace will not attract. It will repel. It does the very thing Jesus went out of his way to say he did not come to do, which was to condemn the world. Grace without truth will not transform lives, for it offers little to the world it does not already have. A truthless grace is little more than an attempt to superficially relieve a person's guilt or to provide a safe environment where they will be accepted and not judged. You can get either one of those from a secular counseling session. Or from a good bartender, for that matter. Either approach can attract large crowds and ardent fans, because both approaches have an ample base among consumer-minded Christians. But for reaching the unchurched, neither has immediate (in the case of truth without grace) or lasting (in the case of grace without truth) appeal.

What the world needs are churches that unapologetically proclaim the full truth of the Christian faith while working hard to build relational bridges to those they are trying to reach. We need churches that enable people to realize that yes, they are broken, but yes, they are also beloved. We need churches that bring both truth and grace.

DRYING OFF

The ultimate mark of a church for the unchurched is this: it is filled with people who continually remember their former lostness. They never forget their baptism and how desperately they needed it. And well they should remember. Nothing is more moving, more meaningful, more inspiring, more invigorating to me than a baptism. A life that has been changed emerges from the water publicly confessing Jesus as forgiver and leader. They are forever marked, forever changed.

Their marriage will never be the same.

Their parenting will never be the same.

Their self-esteem, sense of purpose, values system, code of conduct, investment in community, and sense of vocation and calling will never be the same.

And most of all, their eternity will never be the same.

I recall having a conversation with a member of our staff and lamenting how some Christians forget the effort that was made on their behalf to bring them to Christ. They turn away from the mission that resulted in their faith. Instead of dying to themselves for the sake of reaching others the way someone had died to themselves for the sake of reaching them, they fell to the spiritual narcissism so prevalent in our day. Then out came a sentence I hadn't articulated before but had long viscerally felt: "Some people dry off after their baptism."

Though once they couldn't wait to tell their friends about Christ, now they purposefully have few (if any) non-Christian friends and no sense of urgency about the state of the lost.

Though once they praised the outward focus of the church that brought them to Christ, now they complain about it not meeting their needs, feeding their spiritual stomachs, or serving their spiritual self-interests.

Though once they celebrated every lost coin found, lost sheep recovered, and prodigal son returned, now they are like the older brother who wonders why their father isn't throwing a party for them.

The loss of passion for, commitment to, and urgency about the mission isn't all that can fade after baptism, but it's the bitterest irony for me. If only we could all remember how far we once were from God (Eph. 2:13) and how serious it is to forget our first love (Rev. 2:4).

I wish that no one would ever dry off.

THINKING

STRATEGICALLY

16

What Business
Are You In?

Babies are our business, our only business.
—GERBER BABY FOOD[1]

Have you heard of the "death by iPhone" syndrome? It's the way
the iPhone has functionally killed or dramatically removed various things from the cultural scene. Maps: world atlases, guidebooks, globes, and the old foldable paper maps of cities, states, and countries that were once ubiquitous. These are no longer needed thanks to apps such as Google Maps or Waze. Point-and-shoot cameras: (many of you reading this can't even imagine such a device!) now used solely by dedicated photographers. Recent iPhones have a built-in camera that takes higher-quality pictures than high-end professional cameras did only a few decades ago. The iPhone even eliminated the iPod. If you still have a wallet, you might want to take a picture of it to show your kids or grandkids one day, because your phone will soon replace it if it hasn't already. In a matter of cultural seconds, we will undoubtedly be paying for most

if not all of our goods and services digitally with our phones instead of with plastic cards.[2]

So was there any hope for the mapmakers of the world to stay not only employed but relevant? Of course. If they had been able to see what business they were truly in, they would have been the ones to lead the way in the digital world. But cartographers simply kept producing maps on paper, thinking that was their business, and retailers kept their map stores and sold paper maps until they finally went out of business.

This simple idea of knowing what business you are in is one of the most important for the church as it attempts to engage our post-Christian, digital world. Change is happening at too fast a pace for the church to be anything other than nimble with tactics and clear on strategies. We have to know what business we are in and adapt to change accordingly.

TRAINS AND TRANSPORTATION

In the late 1800s, no business matched the financial and political importance of the railroad. Trains dominated the transportation industry of the United States, moving both people and goods throughout the country. Then a new discovery came along—the car—and incredibly, the leaders of the railroad industry did not take advantage of their position to participate in that pivotal development. The automotive revolution was happening all around them, and they did not use their industry dominance to take hold of the opportunity. In his seminar based on his bestselling book, *The Search for Excellence*, Tom Peters points out the reason: the railroad barons didn't understand what business they were in. Peters observes that "they thought they were in the train business. But they were in fact in the transportation business. Time passed them by, as did opportunity. They couldn't see what their real purpose was."[3]

They were not the first, nor would they be the last, to make this mistake.

Phrases like "I need a xerox of this" or "Xerox this for me, will you?" once were as ubiquitous as "Google it" is today. To xerox was to make a copy on a photocopying machine. When Xerox's photocopying machine was introduced in 1959, the "Xerox machine" was considered as cutting-edge as the iPhone in 2007. "But just as Xerox made carbon paper obsolete," noted Steve Lohr and Carlos Tejada in the *New York Times*, "the iPhone, Google Docs and the cloud made Xerox a company of the past." After 115 years as an independent business, Xerox combined operations with Fujifilm Holdings of Japan, signaling the end of a company that was once an American icon.[4]

What happened?

"Xerox is a poster child for monopoly technology businesses that cannot make the transition to a new generation of technology," says David B. Yoffie, a professor at the Harvard Business School. Xerox isn't alone. It joins fellow tech companies like Kodak and BlackBerry that "lost the innovation footrace." Or more to the point, Xerox fell into the "competency trap," where an organization "becomes so good at one thing, it can't learn to do anything new."[5] But I would argue the breakdown was more foundational. Xerox thought they were in the paper copying business. In reality, they were in the copying and storage of information business. Paper was secondary to that end. If they had known that, we might still be saying, "I need to xerox this," and it would mean sending it into the cloud.

GIDEONS, HOTELS, CARTS, AND DONUTS

Then there are those organizations that have an epiphany about their true purpose just in time to save their future. What is the business of a hotel? Most would think it is to provide a traveler with overnight accommodations. But is that the deepest answer? When people stopped traveling during the COVID-19 pandemic, the Accor hotel chain realized that they were actually in the "provide a space" business and began offering their rooms for day rentals to people working at home who needed a place with a desk, food, and internet access—all within social and safety guidelines—to get away from the noise and distractions at home. They called it their "hotel office" option.[6]

Then there is the Steele Canvas company. Their factory in Chelsea, Massachusetts, had a booming business making canvas-and-steel storage carts that customers used to stash tools, construction materials, and other items. When the pandemic kicked in, orders dried up and the company was pushed into crisis mode. Just as it was being forced to consider furloughing its seventy employees, it asked anew that one, simple question: "What business are we in?" They realized they weren't in the cart-making business. They were in the manufacturing business. They switched from manufacturing carts to manufacturing masks. Result? They were able to keep their entire staff employed and even had to hire additional workers.[7]

This brings us to donuts. Dunkin' Donuts made an astute move. They dropped *Donuts* from their name. They became known simply as Dunkin'. Why? Because they are about more than donuts. Much more. Most of their business comes from beverages, and by dropping *Donuts* from their name, they could freely pursue being "beverage led." Also, they leave their pivot foot in place in case (more likely when) they become no longer beverage led anymore. Who knows what the future will hold? Right now, 58 percent of their sales are beverages. In years to come, 58 percent of their sales could be bagels. They just don't know. That's why in 2011, Starbucks Coffee became just Starbucks. Then-CEO Howard Schultz noted, "It's possible we'll have other products with our name on it and no coffee in it." Even Weight Watchers became WW, opening up a new mission that is less focused on dieting and more focused on health and wellness.[8]

Religious organizations have also embraced this rethinking. Quick, what do the Gideons do? Many would say, "Put Bibles in hotels." Now imagine that the organization that prints and distributes Bibles to hotels suddenly finds that the hotels are saying, "No, thanks." That's exactly what happened. The Gideons quickly realized that Scripture distribution was never meant to be their main focus. The organization wanted to win people to Christ. Bibles in hotels were just a means to an end. They never were in the "put Bibles in hotels" business, or even the Scripture-distribution business. They were in the evangelism business.[9]

SUNDAY SCHOOL

Knowing what business you're in is no less important in ministry.

As I mentioned, for a short time following my graduate studies, I worked for the Baptist Sunday School Board of the Southern Baptist Convention (SBC) as its leadership consultant for preaching and worship. The board was the catchall agency of the nation's largest Protestant denomination for all things local church—preaching, worship, church growth, discipleship, and, of course, Sunday school. But did you notice something odd about that list? All were aspects of the mission of the church, but only one—Sunday school—was a program or method. And yet it was in the name of the agency.

Why? Because it was a method or program that had become enshrined to the level of orthodoxy.

My job was to study the fastest-growing and most-effective churches and then to teach about my findings to other churches. I used to joke that it was the seminary education nobody gets in seminary. During my short tenure, I published a book on my findings titled *Opening the Front Door: Worship and Church Growth*. It was a controversial book at the time, endorsed by renegade outsiders few had heard of. (Rick Warren, who at the time was still a young church planter whose church was meeting at Trabuco Hills High School in Mission Viejo, California, wrote the foreword.)

It was controversial for a reason.

The premise was simple: weekend worship services had eclipsed traditional age-graded Sunday school in weekend attendance (and had since 1971) and were now the front door of the church. As a result, Sunday at 11:00 a.m. needed fresh attention to ensure it was an open door to the unchurched. Sunday school was not the wave of the future nor what fueled the fastest-growing churches. Weekend services were.

Today? A tame and mainstream idea. Then? Oh my.

The Sunday-school mindset, even in the early 1990s, was pervasive, particularly in the SBC: Want to grow your church? Sunday school. Want to disciple believers? Sunday school. Want to increase steward-ship? Sunday school. Want to end global warming? Sunday school.

My ideas were deeply resisted. Turf wars were waged. Programs and curriculums and jobs had to be protected. Entire livelihoods were based on Sunday school programs, Sunday school curriculums, and Sunday school conferences. As a result, "doing church" a certain way became more important than doing church the most effective way. Those who knew how to do church through a Sunday-school-centric method, and believed deeply in it, became threatened by any other method. Today, the Baptist Sunday School Board does not exist. They changed their name to something more mainstream: Lifeway Christian Resources.

They finally got it.

WHAT BUSINESS ARE *YOU* IN?

So what business are *you* in? I can tell you what businesses you are not in. Just like Dunkin' isn't in the donut business but the food and beverage business, you're not in the Sunday school business, the Awana business, the Upward Sports business, the Men's Fraternity business, the Catalyst business, or any other programmatic business. Let's dive deeper: you're also not in the small group business, women's ministry business, men's ministry business, or any other subministry business. All of these may be well and good and helpful, but they are not your business and should not be treated as such.

Do you know what business you're in?

Jim Collins, one of the best thinkers on business, organization, and leadership, has suggested that to really get to the heart of your purpose, you should ask at least five sequential "why" questions. Posit what you do, such as "I own and operate a gas station." Then ask yourself why. And then, with every answer, ask yourself why again and then again. At least five times. Or as Collins suggests, "Start with the statement, 'We make X products' and then ask 'why' five times. . . . After five whys, you'll find that you're getting to the fundamental purpose of the business."[10]

Have you ever done this with the church? Instead of "We make X products," let's start off with "We are building a church."

1. Why are we building a church? *To engage the cause of Christ.*
2. Why are we engaging the cause of Christ? *The world needs Jesus.*
3. Why does the world need Jesus? *People are dead in their sin and face an eternity in hell.*
4. Why are they still dead in their sin and facing an eternity in hell? *They have not entered into a relationship with God through the work of Jesus on the cross.*
5. Why have they not entered into a relationship with God through the work of Jesus on the cross if they so desire? *They haven't been told or they don't know how.*

So what is the primary purpose of the church?

There are many answers, and the most theologically rounded would be the fivefold answer of worship, ministry, evangelism, community, and discipleship. But if you want to keep drilling down through the five whys and move from answering purpose to getting laser sharp on mission, it would be telling people who don't know about Jesus all about Jesus.

TURNING THE FLYWHEEL

In his monograph to accompany his book *Good to Great*, Collins talks about "turning the flywheel." His research on companies that went from good to great discovered that there was "no single defining action, no grand program, no single killer innovation, no solitary lucky break, no miracle moment." What did mark the great companies? They kept pushing at things as if they were pushing a giant, heavy flywheel. "Pushing with great effort, you get the flywheel to inch forward. You keep pushing, and with persistent effort, you get the flywheel to complete one entire turn. You don't stop. You keep pushing. The flywheel moves a bit faster. Two turns . . . then four . . . then eight . . . the flywheel builds momentum . . . sixteen . . . thirty-two . . . moving faster . . . a thousand . . . ten thousand . . . a hundred thousand. Then at some point—breakthrough! The flywheel flies forward with almost unstoppable momentum."[11]

Applying this concept to Amazon, Jeff Bezos and his team determined that the flywheel that powered their business was low prices. As Brad Stone outlines in *The Everything Store*, the lower the prices, the more people would visit their site. With added customers, they add sales as well as third-party sellers. This enabled Amazon to get more out of fixed costs like the fulfillment centers, not to mention the servers needed to run the website. All this in turn led to even lower prices. "Feed any part of this flywheel, they reasoned, and it should accelerate the loop."[12] So the principle is clear: push the flywheel at the points that power your business and keep pushing—over and over and over.

What is the church's flywheel? What business are we in? Where do we push? Our overarching purpose is worship, ministry, evangelism, community, and discipleship. We are in the business of evangelizing the lost, assimilating the evangelized, discipling the assimilated, and unleashing the discipled. It has been that way for nearly two thousand years. The flywheel is clear.

The Flywheel of the Church
FIGURE 16.1

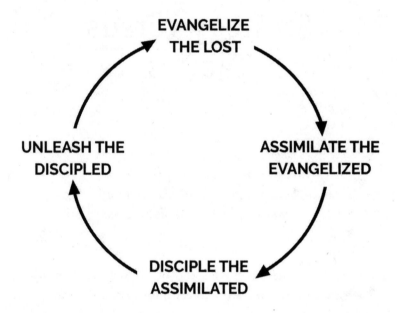

Once we understand this—deeply, viscerally—then we are able to engage in what is arguably the most important discipline in an ever-changing world: becoming strategic in our thinking, particularly in light of tactics.

Strategy versus Tactics

The most promising words ever written
on the maps of human knowledge are
"terra incognita"—unknown territory.
—DANIEL BOORSTIN, *THE DISCOVERERS*[1]

Strategy, in the military, is the science of directing large-scale operations, such as maneuvering forces into the most advantageous position prior to engagement with the enemy. It's a skill rooted in planning and managing. Tactics are literally "matters of arrangement." Again, in a military context, it is the science of arranging forces in view of short-range objectives. Tactics are methods used to achieve an end. So strategy lies behind when and where (and even whether) to use armed conflict to achieve an objective; tactics dictate battlefield maneuvers. Obviously, both are important and intertwined. But in their intertwining is where countless mistakes are made.

Many organizations, and many churches, often make two critical mistakes. First, they treat tactics as if they are strategy. For example, take small groups. It should not be any church's strategy to have small groups. Small groups are a tactic. The strategy is to be a biblically functioning community that practices the "one anothers." Small groups are simply a means to that end and may or may not even be the best means to that end.

Or consider a multisite approach to church growth. Though it's often called a strategy, it's not. It's a tactic. A strategy is to grow your church through the unchurched in your community. Having additional physical campuses is simply one way of pursuing that strategy. But the goal is not to be a multisite church. That is a tactic that should be embraced only if it's important to the strategy. When you confuse a tactic with strategy, the tactic becomes sacrosanct. Soon the goal is to preserve the tactic rather than to pursue the strategy. Tactics exist only to serve the strategy. You should ruthlessly evaluate whether they continue to serve the strategy.

A second mistake is to employ a set of tactics without having a strategy. This is when you have a number of activities, but no plan for what you are trying to achieve, much less how these activities work together to achieve it. You're expending lots of energy and generating lots of activity, but all you have are a disjointed collection of energized activities. Many dire consequences flow from this mistake, but two stand out. First, nothing is aligned for impact. Think of light. Diffused light doesn't make much of a difference, but focus it with a magnifying glass and you can set something on fire. Focus it even more, and it becomes a laser you can use to cut through sheet metal. Tactics without a strategy is diffused light; tactics with a strategy is a laser beam. A second consequence is that without a strategy, you can't evaluate what you should be doing and, often more important, what you should not be doing.

We will never rise to meet the challenges of our day until we extricate ourselves from ineffective methods of ministry and outreach, discipleship and community. But even more important, we must grow in our awareness of what is a tactic and what is a strategy—and knowing what business we are in. Meeting the challenges of ministry in a post-Christian, digital age requires so many changes and pivots, rethinkings and retoolings that the most important tool in our toolbox is strategic thinking.

Our mantra should be that while the mission, vision, values, and message of the church are timeless and unchanging, we must continuously evaluate the effectiveness of our methods. Whether we're confusing tactics with strategy or employing tactics without strategy, the lesson is the same: get strategic.

WHY WE ENDED OUR MULTISITE APPROACH

In 2019, just before the pandemic that no one knew was coming, we closed all of our satellite campuses and ended the multisite approach to growth we had embraced for nearly a decade. This made more than a few waves at the time and was even picked up by many Christian news sites. It flew in the face of a hot church trend.

The multisite model is not complicated to understand. The goal, at least for us, was never to simply make it more convenient for current "Meckers" to attend. The goal was to break down geographic barriers that might inhibit an unchurched person from considering an invitation to attend Meck to explore what Jesus might mean for their life. We decided to chart a different course. It wasn't because our sites were failing. They weren't. Most were growing. It wasn't because the church as a whole was in decline. We were coming off a record season of growth and a year in which we'd had hundreds of baptisms.

So why did we end our multisite approach?

We were committed to tirelessly evaluating our methods for missional effectiveness. This evaluation means asking not only whether our methods are still working but how well they are working. And perhaps most important, it means asking how their effectiveness compares with the potential effectiveness of other methods. If we find that a method is wanting or that there is a better method to use, then no matter what that method is, no matter what the optics might be, no matter how much time and money and effort has been invested in that method, the method has to go.

We decided that it was time to end the multisite approach and to invest our resources and efforts more strategically because to reach a post-Christian world, "It's the internet, stupid."

The multisite approach is a physical approach in a digital world. Even worse, it's a physical response to a digital demand. As Carey Nieuwhof quipped in one of his blogs, "The internet is the venue in which the entire community you are trying to reach lives."[2]

We were finding that when people were invited by a friend, instead of attending a physical campus, they first visited our website or some other online venture, and then—as a secondary step—attended one of our online campus services. Our attenders even intuitively recommended that process to them. It wasn't long before our online campus became our fastest-growing and second-largest venue. (It is now our largest.) As we saw earlier, the new front door of the church is not a physical place. It's digital. The role of the multisite approach was to remove geographical barriers. Today, those are not the barriers that need to be removed. The unchurched do not begin with geography. They begin online.

Many strategists maintain that people will not travel more than fifteen to twenty minutes from home to attend a church. Ironically, the multisite approach proves this dictum's obsolescence. The multisite approach is based on a church having a regional appeal that allows it to establish a campus outside of that mythical twenty-minute window because they already have people commuting from more than twenty minutes away. People *will* travel to attend a church they are attracted to and have come to experience and value.

In a predigital world, it was only the initial invitation that was thwarted by the twenty-minute rule, because it involved physical attendance. But in a digital age, people can and even want to explore a church from the comfort, privacy, and anonymity of their homes. Once they are intrigued by a church online, they think little of driving to experience what they saw online, even if it takes more than twenty minutes to get there.

In the final stages of our months-long evaluation of the multisite approach, we randomly surveyed nearly a thousand of our attenders and found several confirming realities: (1) they were inviting friends to our original campus instead of our newer campuses no matter where they lived; (2) if they weren't inviting their friends to the original campus, they were inviting them to our online experiences or to listen to a week-end message on our app; (3) no matter where they lived in Charlotte, they didn't feel that the campuses near them were needed for reaching their unchurched friends; and (4) they were most comfortable inviting their friends to non-video-venue events and services. (Like most multisite churches, our worship and children's ministry were "live," but used video for the message.)

We were putting a tool in our attenders' hands that they didn't ask for, didn't feel was needed, and didn't use—at least for the mission. They may have attended one of the sites out of convenience or a sense of duty, but they didn't use it for their unchurched friends. We gave them the physical, but they voted with their feet for the digital.

So for us, it was a missional decision many months in the making and made from a position of health. But that's not all. Ending the multisite approach freed up resources we could funnel into methods we had become convinced would be far more effective at turning the flywheel. We dreamed of expanding our digital footprint, making our website so much more than it was (particularly making it work seamlessly with mobile technology), using social media and digital marketing to reach out in unprecedented ways, staffing our online campus as if it were a physical campus, expanding our video-production capabilities, and so much more.

So in one sense, we're still multisite. It's just that one is physical and the other is digital.

We continue to celebrate that decision. Not simply because we were more than ready when the pandemic hit and the world was thrown online but because even before COVID, our online growth became meteoric and even our in-person services grew.

EMOTIONAL BUT RATIONAL

Such decisions are not easy. They are emotional. They can also be affected by sin. I recall more than one moment when I resisted shutting down the sites and moving to digital because having multiple sites had become such a badge of ministerial pride for me. In the end, that resistance was laid bare for the pride that it was, and I became more resolved than ever to think strategically.

But that doesn't mean there wasn't emotion involved. There was. When making such decisions, there always is.

IKEA recently engaged in a stunningly strategic move. As reported by *Inc.*, "After seventy years, hundreds of millions of copies, and countless hours of inspiration to armchair interior designers . . . [IKEA] has decided to kill its beloved catalog."[3] In a statement, the company said, "Over the years [the catalog] has become an iconic and beloved publication, and it has been an important success factor for IKEA to reach and inspire many people across the world." And then these telling words: "But times are changing. IKEA has become more digital and accessible while embracing new ways to connect with more people. Customer behavior and media consumption has changed, and the IKEA Catalog has been less used. [IKEA has] therefore taken the emotional but rational decision to respectfully end the successful career of the IKEA Catalog, both the print and digital versions—and look to the future with excitement."[4]

It's hard to end something successful that you created and invested in (and that you likely are emotionally attached to) because you are astute enough to realize that it has run its course. That may be the single hardest thing a leader can actualize. Note the four words IKEA used to describe its decision: it was an "emotional but rational decision." Yes, such decisions always are. And it's critical to understand the dynamic between the emotional and the rational. It's not like saying, "We used to ship by FedEx, but now will be going with UPS." It's more like saying, "We are ending a way of doing things, a shared experience we have fond memories of, and venturing into an emotional vacuum."

Emotion is why such decisions are seldom made, and why when they are made, they are so fiercely resisted. It's simply too easy to reject "emotional but rational" and cling to "emotional." Why? For church members:

- You're not just closing a site, you're ending a community.
- You're not just ending Sunday school, you're changing what "going to church" on Sundays has meant to them.
- You're not just moving to a new location, you're taking away the building they gave money to construct and all that took place when they met there.
- You're not just changing the music, you're changing how they worship and taking away the songs they love.
- You're not just going online, you're changing what it means to attend.
- You're not just . . .

Well, you get it.

Imagine how emotional it must have been for IKEA to end a catalog that was first put together in 1951 by the founder, Ingvar Kamprad. At IKEA's peak in 2016, it distributed two hunded million copies in thirty-two languages. But notice, again, their reasoning: "But times are changing. IKEA has become more digital and accessible while embracing new ways to connect with more people. Customer behavior and media consumption has changed, and the IKEA Catalog has been less used." That is an understatement. IKEA's worldwide online retail sales increased by 45 percent in 2019 alone. That was prepandemic. They needed to pivot, along with the rest of the retail world, to a digital strategy that includes a "continuously improving company website, a suite of apps and social media." The resources once used to promote the catalog were much better spent in new and more strategic ways. That is the rational speaking to the emotional, which is the heart of emotional intelligence.

What if more church leaders (and the people in their churches) chose emotional intelligence over mere emotion? What if they made more "emotional but rational" decisions regarding ministry, outreach, and organization? What if they looked at the digital revolution that has taken place and reevaluated previous strategies?

Our decision to end our multisite approach was a watershed moment. It was made during our annual budget-development process, when we needed to bring all that we wanted to do in line with our best projections of what we could actually spend. We are conservative on fiscal matters, so this is never a small exercise.

I had long been wrestling with our sites' effectiveness as an outreach tool compared with the potential the digital revolution offered. Suddenly, in those budget meetings, the two investments came into stark contrast: we were locked in to spending enormous amounts of money on facility rental and staff-intensive weekend services at various locations around the city, which didn't leave us the resources we needed to improve our website, invest in digital marketing, take our app to a new level, and make our online campus state of the art. Like never before, I was confronted by the conflict between where our money was going and where it could go. Having to say no to what I knew would bear even more fruit than our expensive sites made me want to throw up in the corner. But close the sites? The emotional was running headlong into the rational.

I decided then and there. To continue to invest in a less effective strategy would prohibit us from investing in a better strategy. The rational must win, no matter the emotional cost.

Here are three key lessons for leaders:

1. The times are always changing. You don't change your methods just once, and then you are set for a lengthy season of doing things the same way. The times are *always* changing. What works now will almost certainly not be what will work then.
2. You must acknowledge that you have emotional attachments that can cloud your objectivity. Please reread that sentence.
3. Emotional intelligence is acknowledging the emotion involved but letting the facts speak to the matter and then making the hard, necessary "emotional but rational" decisions that will ensure your ongoing vibrancy.

As Adam Grant explored in his book *Think Again*, which we talked about in the introduction, we must not simply think and learn but rethink and unlearn.[5]

Afterword

We should all be concerned about
the future because we will have to
spend the rest of our lives there.
—CHARLES F. KETTERING¹

It was a disturbing headline: "Church of Canada May Disappear by 2040, Says New Report." It was being forecast "that there will be no members, attenders or givers in the Anglican Church of Canada by approximately 2040."² This was said by Neil Elliot, who authored the report commissioned by the church and delivered an address to the Council of General Synod in Ontario.

The report was based on five different methodologies of analysis, all giving the same dire prediction. The freefall that had already taken place is stunning. Membership in the Anglican Church had fallen from a high of 1.3 million in 1961 to just more than 357,000 in 2017.³ While there were many appropriate reactions to the report, including calls for the church to put forward a more robust and creative witness for Christ, one rector took solace in the words of former Archbishop of Canterbury Rowan Williams, who once said that "the church is not ours to save." Reflecting on the statement, the rector concluded, "We are only called to be good stewards of what we have been given. God will do what God will do."⁴

If that thinking rules the day, the prediction of the death of the Canadian Anglican Church will come true. Why? Because it is among the deadliest of theologies when put forward and applied in this manner. Of course, in the broad theological context that I am confident Williams meant, the church is *not* ours to save. But the erroneous application of it and the sentiment that was drawn from it is so wrong. Yes, God is going to do what God is going to do, but what God has willed to do is to work through his people! There is no room for a passive fatalism when it comes to the work and expansion of the church. This generation of Christians will give an account to God for its outreach to people who are outside of the church.

Period.

A telling verse from the great wisdom book of the Bible says, "The horse is made ready for the day of battle, but victory rests with the LORD" (Prov. 21:31). Yes, the victory is always the Lord's; we do not put our trust in horses. But it *is* our responsibility to ready the horse for the contest. If we don't, we are not inviting the Lord's victory. It is akin to Augustine's adage about praying as if it all depends on God, but then working as if it all depends on you.

I hope the Anglican Church in Canada turns things around. I hope they regain their evangelical moorings. I hope they risk creativity and innovation in their evangelistic efforts. I hope they pray and fast. But I also hope they will not give way to an insidious theology that removes the responsibility and urgency to do *something* in the face of their stunning decline.

Because that is not what God would have them do.

And that is my prayer for you. I know that much of what you've read in this book may have felt overwhelming. You may have felt a great temptation not to engage with it at all.

I understand.

I just celebrated my sixtieth birthday, which means I'm not exactly a digital native. I was still using a typewriter when I started graduate school, and only during my PhD studies did a "word processor" become a part of my life. Shortly after I planted the church I have now led for more than thirty years, my assistant begged me to think about using something she called "email" for our correspondence. At the time, it sounded absurd, and I would have none of it.

But I adapted to the digital world. And embraced it. And I'm so glad. Because the mission matters—a mission that is filled with real people, real names, real families, and real eternities. And I can't imagine a better way to end than with the experience of one of those very real people:

As I was watching the online service of Mecklenburg Community Church and their reflection on this past year, I was reflecting on how much Meck has impacted and influenced my life in the three short years I've been attending.

Because of Meck, my husband and I have become Christians.

Because of Meck, my husband and I were baptized.

Because of Meck, our marriage has been strengthened.

Because of Meck, my gift and passion that he gave me for dancing has been used to serve him.

Because of Meck, I'm disovering and transforming into the woman that God made me to be.

I am so proud and incredibly grateful to call Meck my church home and I know God will continue to strengthen and transform me through this church to further his mission. Thank you, @ meckchurch.

4 likes

As I was watching the online service of Mecklenburg Community Church and their reflection on the past year, I was reflecting on how much Meck has impacted and influenced my life in the 3 short years I've been attending.

Because of Meck, my husband and I have become Christians.
Because of Meck, my husband and I were baptized.
Because of Meck, our marriage has been strengthened.
Because of Meck, my gift and passion that He gave me for dancing has been used to serve him.
Because of Meck, I'm discovering and transforming into the woman that God made me to be.

I am so proud and incredibly grateful to call Meck my church home and I know God will continue to strengthen and transform me through this church to further His mission. Thank you, @meckchurch

View all comments

2 hours ago

Notes

INTRODUCTION

1. Cited by historian David McCullough, *The Greater Journey: Americans in Paris* (New York: Simon and Schuster, 2011), 267. Washburne was the twenty-fifth United States secretary of state and the American minister to France from 1869 to 1877.

2. Centers for Disease Control and Prevention, "A Tragic Milestone," COVID Data Tracker Weekly Review, May 13, 2022, www.cdc.gov /coronavirus/2019-ncov/covid-data/covidview/past-reports/05132022 .html.

3. Patrick Van Kessel et al., "In Their Own Words, Americans Describe the Struggles and Silver Linings of the COVID-19 Pandemic," Pew Research Center, March 5, 2021, www.pewresearch.org/2021/03/05/in-their-own -words-americans-describe-the-struggles-and-silver-linings-of-the-covid -19-pandemic/.

4. Yonat Shimron, "Study: Attendance Hemorrhaging at Small and Midsize US Congregations," Religious News Network, October 14, 2021, https://religionnews.com/2021/10/14/study-attendance-at-small -and-midsize-us-congregations-is-hemorrhaging/; Janet Adamy, "Churches Changed during the Pandemic and Many Aren't Going Back," *Wall Street Journal*, November 12, 2021, www.wsj.com/articles /church-pandemic-covid-online-11636728162. See also Kate Shellnutt, "Southern Baptists Drop 1.1. Million Members in Three Years," *Christianity Today*, May 12, 2022, www.christianitytoday.com/news /2022/may/southern-baptist-membership-decline-covid-pandemic -baptisms.html.

5. Aaron Earls, "Livestreaming Services Hasn't Been an Option for Many Churches," Lifeway Research, March 16, 2020, https://research.lifeway.com/2020/03/16/livestreaming-services-hasnt-been-an-option-for-many-churches/.

6. Ibid.

7. Aaron Earls, "Online Services Expanded Reach of Churches During Pandemic," Lifeway Research, October 14, 2021, https://research.lifeway.com/2021/10/14/online-services-expanded-reach-of-churches-during-pandemic/.

8. Andrew Conrad, "Ten Powerful Church Statistics on Social Media Use," Capterra, March 13, 2018, https://blog.capterra.com/church-statistics-social-media/.

9. Adam Grant, *Think Again: The Power of Knowing What You Don't Know* (New York: Viking, 2021), 19.

10. Ibid., 19–20.

11. Ibid., 20.

12. Ibid., 30.

13. This is a proverb from the fourteenth century, literally "he who sups with the devil should have a long spoon." Elizabeth Knowles, *The Oxford Dictionary of Phrase and Fable* (Oxford: Oxford Univ. Press, 2005), www.oxfordreference.com/view/10.1093/acref/9780198609810.001.0001/acref-9780198609810-e-6866.

CHAPTER 1: FROM CHRISTIAN TO POST-CHRISTIAN

1. Francis X. Rocca, "Pope Francis, in Christmas Message, Says Church Must Adapt to Post-Christian West," *Wall Street Journal*, December 21, 2019, www.wsj.com/articles/pope-francis-in-christmas-message-says-church-must-adapt-to-post-christian-west-11576930226.

2. For a fuller and more detailed evaluation of the nature of the Christian world, from the Middle Ages to the Enlightenment, see James Emery White, *Serious Times: Making Your Life Matter in an Urgent Day* (Downers Grove, IL: Intervarsity, 2005), from which this section has been adapted.

3. On this, see Marcia L. Colish, *Medieval Foundations of the Western Intellectual Tradition: 400–1400*, Yale Intellectual History of the West (New Haven, CT: Yale Univ. Press, 1997).

4. Johan Huizinga, *The Autumn of the Middle Ages*, trans. Rodney J.

Payton and Ulrich Mammitzsch (1919; Chicago: Univ. of Chicago Press, 1996), 174.

5. Norman F. Cantor, *The Civilization of the Middle Ages: A Completely Revised and Expanded Edition of* Medieval History: The Life and Death of a Civilization (1963; New York: HarperCollins, 1993), 21.

6. Jeffrey Burton Russell, *A History of Medieval Christianity: Prophecy and Order* (Arlington Heights, IL: Harlan Davidson, 1968), 83.

7. Martin Marty, *A Short History of Christianity*, 2nd ed. (Philadelphia: Fortress, 1987), 75.

8. See Mark A. Noll, *Turning Points: Decisive Moments in the History of Christianity* (Grand Rapids: Baker; Leicester: InterVarsity, 1997), 121.

9. Ibid., 122.

10. Fernand Braudel, *A History of Civilizations*, trans. Richard Mayne (New York: Penguin, 1994), 341.

11. On this, see J. I. Packer and Thomas Howard, *Christianity: The True Humanism* (Waco: Word, 1985).

12. See Alister E. McGrath, "Humanism and the Reformation," in *Reformation Thought: An Introduction* (Oxford: Basil Blackwell, 1988), 27–49.

13. Francis A. Schaeffer, *Escape from Reason* (Downers Grove, IL: Intervarsity, 1968).

14. Christian Smith, "Introduction: Rethinking the Secularization of American Public Life," in *The Secular Revolution: Power, Interests, and Conflict in the Secularization of American Public Life*, ed. Christian Smith (Berkeley: Univ. of California Press, 2003), 5.

15. Alexis de Tocqueville, *The Old Regime and the French Revolution*, trans. Stuart Gilbert (1856; Garden City, NY: Doubleday, 1955), 149.

16. As cited by Emmet Kennedy, *A Cultural History of the French Revolution* (New Haven, CT: Yale Univ. Press, 1989), 343. The hymn was composed by Chenier, with music by Gossec.

17. Peter L. Berger, ed., *The Desecularization of the World: Resurgent Religion and World Politics* (Washington, DC: Ethics and Public Policy Center; Grand Rapids: Eerdmans, 1999), 2.

18. On this, see Huston Smith, *Why Religion Matters: The Fate of the Human Spirit in an Age of Disbelief* (New York: HarperSanFrancisco, 2001), 103.

19. For a deeper dive into these four marks, see White, *Serious Times*, from which this section has been somewhat adapted.

20. These four marks were first suggested to my thinking by Langdon Gilkey in *Naming the Whirlwind: The Renewal of God-Language* (Indianapolis: Bobbs-Merril, 1969), and again in a variant form by Thomas C. Oden's *After Modernity . . . What? Agenda for Theology* (Grand Rapids: Zondervan, 1990). I have used Oden's terms over Gilkey's, which speak of the Geist of the modern secular world in terms of contingency, relativism, temporality, and autonomy.

21. Allan Bloom, *The Closing of the American Mind: How Higher Education Has Failed Democracy and Impoverished the Souls of Today's Students* (New York: Simon and Schuster, 1987), 25.

22. Jean-Paul Sartre, *Existentialism and Human Emotions* (New York: Citadel, 1957), 63.

23. Jacques Barzun, *From Dawn to Decadence: 500 Years of Western Cultural Life; 1500 to the Present* (New York: HarperCollins, 2000), xv.

24. Oden, *After Modernity . . . What?* 74, cf. 157. Italics in original.

25. Steve Bruce, *Religion in the Modern World: From Cathedrals to Cults* (Oxford: Oxford Univ. Press, 1996), 5.

26. Anjana Ahuja, "God Is Not in Charge, We Are," *Times*, July 24, 2003, 6.

27. Christopher Lasch, *The Culture of Narcissism: American Life in an Age of Diminishing Expectations* (1979; New York: Norton, 1991), 7.

28. Stanley J. Grenz, *A Primer on Postmodernism* (Grand Rapids: Eerdmans, 1996), 62.

29. Tessa Koumoundouros, "There Are Two Types of Narcissist, and the Difference Is Crucial, Research Shows," Science Alert, April 18, 2022, www.sciencealert.com/there-are-actually-two-types-of-narcissist-and-the -difference-is-crucial-researcher-shows.

30. Gerard Piel, *The Age of Science: What Scientists Learned in the Twentieth Century* (New York: Basic Books, 2001).

31. Peter Berger, *The Sacred Canopy* (Garden City, NY: Doubleday, 1969), 107.

32. Ian Barbour, *When Science Meets Religion: Enemies, Strangers, or Partners?* (London: SPCK, 2000), xi.

33. For an informed critique of many of the more popular aspects of applied naturalism, see Phillip E. Johnson, *Reason in the Balance: The Case against Naturalism in Science, Law and Education* (Downers Grove, IL: Intervarsity, 1995).

34. Carl Sagan, *The Demon-Haunted World: Science as a Candle in the Dark* (New York: Random House, 1995).

35. As cited by Owen Chadwick, *The Secularization of the European Mind in the Nineteenth Century* (Cambridge: Cambridge Univ. Press, 1975), 10.

36. Christopher Dawson, *Dynamics of World History*, ed. John J. Mulloy (Wilmington, DE: ISI Books, 2002), xxxi, citing *Enquiries* (London, 1933), vi.

37. Nietzsche's famed "God is dead" passage can be found in section 125 of *The Gay Science*, available in *The Portable Nietzsche*, ed. Walter Kaufmann (New York: Penguin, 1982), 95–96.

CHAPTER 2: THE RISE OF THE NONES

1. Dan Gilgoff, "My Take: Five Things I Learned Editing the Belief Blog," CNN, December 31, 2012, https://religion.blogs.cnn.com/2012/12/31 /my-take-5-things-i-learned-editing-the-belief-blog/.

2. James Emery White, *The Rise of the Nones: Understanding and Reaching the Religiously Unaffiliated* (Grand Rapids: Baker, 2014).

3. Gregory A. Smith, "About Three-in-Ten U.S. Adults Are Now Religiously Unaffiliated," Pew Research Center, December 14, 2021, www.pewforum.org/2021/12/14/about-three-in-ten-u-s-adults-are-now -religiously-unaffiliated/.

4. Betsy Cooper et al., "Exodus: Why Americans are Leaving Religion— and Why They're Unlikely to Come Back," PRRI, September 22, 2016, www.prri.org/research/prri-rns-poll-nones-atheist-leaving -religion/.

5. Jeffrey M. Jones, "U.S. Church Membership Falls below Majority for First Time," Gallup, March 29, 2021, https://news.gallup.com/poll /341963/church-membership-falls-below-majority-first-time.aspx.

6. Aaron Earls, "Protestant Church Closures Outpace Openings in the U.S.," Lifeway Research, May 25, 2021, https://research.lifeway.com /2021/05/25/protestant-church-closures-outpace-openings-in-u-s/.

7. Yonat Shimron, "Study: More Churches Closing Than Opening," Religion News Service, May 26, 2021, https://religionnews.com /2021/05/26/study-more-churches-closing-than-opening/.

8. J. Curtice et al., eds., "British Social Attitudes: The Thirty-Sixth Report," National Centre for Social Research 2019, www.bsa.natcen .ac.uk/media/39293/1_bsa36_religion.pdf.

9. Gabriella Swerling, "Christians Close to Falling below 50pc in England for First Time," *Telegraph*, December 16, 2021, www.telegraph.co.uk

/news/2021/12/16/christianity-close-falling-50-per-cent-england
-first-time/.

10. William Booth and Amanda Ferguson, "Pope Francis Is Set to Visit an
Ireland Where the Catholic Church Is in Steep Decline," *Washington
Post*, August 19, 2018, www.washingtonpost.com/world/europe/the
-pope-is-set-to-visit-an-ireland-where-true-believers-are-in-steep-decline
/2018/08/18/d75cf648-9bed-11e8-a8d8-9b4c13286d6b_story.html.

11. "Being Christian in Western Europe," Pew Research Center, May 29,
2018, www.pewforum.org/2018/05/29/being-christian-in-western
-europe/.

12. "Fifty-One Percent of French Do Not Believe in God, Survey Says,"
Evangelical Focus—Europe, September 29, 2021, https://evangelicalfocus
.com/europe/13460/51-of-french-do-not-believe-in-god-survey-says.

13. Justin McCarthy, "U.S. Confidence in Organized Religion Remains
Low," Gallup, July 8, 2019, https://news.gallup.com/poll/259964
/confidence-organized-religion-remains-low.aspx.

14. "Why America's 'Nones' Don't Identify with a Religion," Pew Research
Center, August 8, 2018, www.pewresearch.org/fact-tank/2018/08/08
/why-americas-nones-dont-identify-with-a-religion/.

CHAPTER 3: POST–CHRISTIAN SPIRITUALITY

1. Robert Bellah et al., *Habits of the Heart: Individualism and Commitment
in American Life* (San Francisco: Harper and Row, 1985), 221.

2. Ross Douthat, "The Overstated Collapse of American Christianity,"
New York Times, October 29, 2019, www.nytimes.com/2019/10/29
/opinion/american-christianity.html.

3. Jessica Bennett, "When Did Everybody Become a Witch?" *New York
Times*, October 24, 2019, www.nytimes.com/2019/10/24/books/peak
-witch.html.

4. Ibid.

5. Brandon Showalter, "Witches Outnumber Presbyterians in the
US; Wicca, Paganism Growing 'Astronomically,'" *Christian Post*,
October 10, 2018, www.christianpost.com/news/witches-outnumber-
presbyterians-in-the-us-wicca-paganism-growing-astronomically
-227857/.

6. Yonat Shimron, "New Poll Finds Even Religious Americans Feel the
Good Vibrations," Religion News Service, August 29, 2018, https://

religionnews.com/2018/08/29/new-poll-finds-even-religious-americans
-feel-the-good-vibrations/.

7. Bennett, "When Did Everybody Become a Witch?"

8. Heather Greene, "Tarot Booms as Generation Z Sorts Out Spiritual
Path," Religion News Service, April 26, 2021, https://religionnews.
com/2021/04/26/tarot-booms-as-generation-z-sorts-out-spiritual-path/.

9. Courtney Kennedy and Arnold Lau, "Most Americans Believe in
Intelligent Life beyond Earth; Few See UFOs as a Major National
Security Threat," Pew Research Center, June 30, 2021, www
.pewresearch.org/fact-tank/2021/06/30/most-americans-believe-in
-intelligent-life-beyond-earth-few-see-ufos-as-a-major-national-security
-threat/.

10. Wikipedia, s.v. "Jedism," last modified June 20, 2022, 21:31, https://
en.wikipedia.org/wiki/Jediism.

11. Diana Walsh Pasulka, *American Cosmic: UFOs, Religion, Technology*
(Oxford: Oxford Univ. Press, 2019), 120.

12. "New Cult: Young Americans Practice Spirituality on TikTok," *TRT
World*, December 24, 2021, www.trtworld.com/magazine/new-cult
-young-americans-practice-spirituality-on-tiktok-52939.

13. Rebecca Jennings, "Is a New Kind of Religion Forming on the Internet?"
Vox, December 14, 2021, www.vox.com/the-goods/22832827
/manifesting-tiktok-astroworld-conspiracy-qanon-religion.

14. Ibid.

15. Ibid.

16. Ibid.

17. Steven D. Smith, *Pagans and Christians in the City: Culture Wars from
the Tiber to the Potomac* (Grand Rapids: Eerdmans, 2018).

18. Peter Leithart, "The Culture Wars Are Ancient History," *Christianity
Today*, November 27, 2018, www.christianitytoday.com/ct/2018
/december/steven-smith-pagans-christians-city-culture-wars.html.

19. Ibid.

20. Megan Brenan, "Birth Control Still Tops List of Morally Acceptable
Issues," Gallup, May 29, 2019, https://news.gallup.com/poll/257858
/birth-control-tops-list-morally-acceptable-issues.aspx.

21. Ibid.

22. Greg Hurst, "Liberal Attitudes on the Rise . . . Unless You're Having an
Affair or in Politics," *Times*, October 24, 2019, www.thetimes.co.uk

/edition/news/liberal-attitudes-on-the-rise-unless-youre-having-an
-affair-or-in-politics-ntbj6ct8r.

23. Francis X. Rocca, "Pope Francis, in Christmas Message, Says Church
Must Adapt to Post-Christian West," *Wall Street Journal*, December 21,
2019, www.wsj.com/articles/pope-francis-in-christmas-message-says
-church-must-adapt-to-post-christian-west-11576930226.

24. Emily Yahr, "'Succession' Season 3 finale: The Five Most Shocking
Moments from a Much-Anticipated Episode," *Washington Post*,
December 13, 2021, www.washingtonpost.com/arts-entertainment
/2021/12/13/succession-season-3-finale-shocking-moments/.

25. "First-Ever Fifty-State Survey on Holocaust Knowledge of American
Millennials and Gen Z Reveals Shocking Results," Claims Conference,
September 16, 2020, www.claimscon.org/millennial-study/.

26. United States Holocaust Memorial Museum, "Introduction to the
Holocaust," Holocaust Encyclopedia, updated November 5, 2021,
https://encyclopedia.ushmm.org/content/en/article/introduction-to
-the-holocaust.

27. Ibid.

28. Kit Ramgopal, "Survey Finds 'Shocking' Lack of Holocaust Knowledge
among Millennials and Gen Z," NBC News, September 16, 2020,
www.nbcnews.com/news/world/survey-finds-shocking-lack-holocaust
-knowledge-among-millennials-gen-z-n1240031.

29. James Emery White, *Meet Generation Z: Understanding and Reaching
the New Post-Christian World* (Grand Rapids: Baker, 2017), 49, 64.

30. Diane Chandler, "State of the Bible: Forty Percent of Gen Z Believe
Jesus Sinned," *Christian Index*, May 10, 2022, https://christianindex.org
/stories/state-of-the-bible-40-percent-of-gen-z-believe-jesus-sinned
,22091.

31. "First-Ever Fifty-State Survey on Holocaust Knowledge."

CHAPTER 4: "WHAT THE H*** HAPPENED IN 2007?"

1. Thomas Friedman, *Thank You for Being Late: An Optimist's Guide
to Thriving in the Age of Accelerations* (New York: Farrar, Straus, and
Giroux, 2016), 25.

2. Wikipedia, s.v. "French Revolution," last modified June 26, 2022, 18:19,
https://en.wikipedia.org/wiki/French_Revolution.

3. Tony Raval, "Digital Transformation in the Age of Millennials and

Gen Z," *Forbes*, August 20, 2019, www.forbes.com/sites
/forbestechcouncil/2019/08/20/digital-transformation-in-the-age-of
-millennials-and-gen-z/#31ea5bfa2708.

4. Eric Schmidt and Jared Cohen, *The New Digital Age: Reshaping the
Future of People, Nations and Business* (New York: Knopf, 2013), 256.

5. Elizabeth Schulze, "Everything You Need to Know about the Fourth
Industrial Revolution," CNBC, January 17, 2019, www.cnbc.com
/2019/01/16/fourth-industrial-revolution-explained-davos-2019.html.

6. Friedman, *Thank You for Being Late*, 20.

7. Nathan Ingraham, "Apple Announces 1 Million Apps in the App Store,
More Than 1 Billion Songs Played on iTunes Radio," *Verge*, October 22,
2013, www.theverge.com/2013/10/22/4866302/apple-announces-1
-million-apps-in-the-app-store.

8. "Mobile App Download Statistics and Usage Statistics (2022),"
Buildfire, https://buildfire.com/app-statistics/.

9. Brian X. Chen, *Always On: How the iPhone Unlocked the Anything-
Anytime-Anywhere Future—and Locked Us In* (Boston: DaCappo, 2011).

10. Knowledge at Wharton Staff, "'Millennials on Steroids': Is Your Brand
Ready for Generation Z?" *Knowledge at Wharton*, September 28, 2015,
http://knowledge.wharton.upenn.edu/article/millennials-on-steroids
-is-your-brand-ready-for-generation-z/.

11. Adrianne Pasquarelli and E. J. Schultz, "Move Over Gen Z, Generation
Alpha Is the One to Watch," *AdAge*, January 22, 2019, https://adage
.com/article/cmo-strategy/move-gen-z-generation-alpha-watch/316314.

12. Joe Drape, "Step Aside, LeBron and Dak, and Make Room for Banjo
and Kazooie," *New York Times*, December 19, 2021, www.nytimes
.com/2021/12/19/sports/esports-fans-leagues-games.html.

13. Leo Sun, "A Foolish Take: How Often Do Americans Use Voice
Assistants?" *Motley Fool*, August 5, 2019, www.fool.com/investing
/2019/08/05/a-foolish-take-how-often-do-americans-use-voice-as.aspx.

14. "The Smart Audio Report," NPR/Edison Research, Spring 2019,
www.nationalpublicmedia.com/uploads/2019/10/The_Smart_Audio
_Report_Spring_2019.pdf.

15. Matthew Field and Tom Hoggins, "5G: The Innovation That Will
Shape All Our Lives for Years to Come," *Telegraph*, July 8, 2019, www
.telegraph.co.uk/technology/2019/07/08/5g-innovation-will-shape
-lives-years-come/.

16. Ibid.

17. Charlie Coombs, "How Gen Z Could Shape the 'Internet of Things,'" *Thred*, February 19, 2020, https://thred.com/change/how-gen-z -could-shape-the-internet-of-things/.

18. Schmidt and Cohen, *New Digital Age*, 5.

19. The Editors, "The Future of Reality," *Wired* 29, no. 12 (December 2021/January 2022), 62–63.

20. Kyle Orland, "So What Is 'the Metaverse,' Exactly?" *Ars Technica*, November 7, 2021, https://arstechnica.com/gaming/2021/11/everyone -pitching-the-metaverse-has-a-different-idea-of-what-it-is.

21. Mike Snider and Brett Molina, "Everyone Wants to Own the Metaverse Including Facebook and Microsoft. But What Exactly Is It?" *USA Today*, November 10, 2021, www.usatoday.com/story/tech/2021/11/10 /metaverse-what-is-it-explained-facebook-microsoft-meta-vr/6337635001/.

22. Ibid.

23. Hubilo, "Hubilo: Five Hot Tech Trends That Will Shape Events in 2022," *BusinessChief*, December 22, 2021, https://businesschief.com /technology-and-ai/hubilo-5-hot-tech-trends-will-shape-events-2022.

24. Orland, "So What Is 'the Metaverse,' Exactly?"

25. Ian Harber and Patrick Miller, "How to Prepare for the Metaverse," *Gospel Coalition*, November 2, 2021, https://www.thegospelcoalition .org/article/prepare-metaverse/.

26. Ibid.

27. David Nield, "What Is Web3 and Why Should You Care?" *Gizmodo*, December 14, 2021, https://gizmodo.com/what-is-web-3-and-why -should-you-care-1848204799.

28. Ibid.

29. Ibid.

30. Mitchell Clark, "NFTs, Explained," *Verge*, August 18, 2021, www .theverge.com/22310188/nft-explainer-what-is-blockchain-crypto -art-faq.

31. Ibid.

32. Max Tegmark, *Life 3.0: Being Human in the Age of Artificial Intelligence* (New York: Knopf, 2017).

33. Ibid., 27–29.

34. Ibid., 37.

35. Marco della Cava, "Elon Musk Says AI Could Doom Human

Civilization. Zuckerberg Disagrees. Who's right?" *USA Today*, January 2, 2018, www.usatoday.com/story/tech/news/2018/01/02/artificial-intelligence-end-world-overblown-fears/985813001/.

36. John Lennox, "Rise of the Machines: New Book Applies Christian Ethics to the Future of AI," interview by Christopher Reese, *Christianity Today*, September 8, 2020, www.christianitytoday.com/ct/2020/september-web-only/john-lennox-2084-ethics-artificial-intelligence.html.

37. Ibid.

38. Ibid.

39. Emily A.Vogels and Monica Anderson, "Americans and Digital Knowledge," Pew Research Center, October 9, 2019, www.pewinternet.org/2019/10/09/americans-and-digital-knowledge/.

40. Quoted in interviews by Friedman, *Thank You for Being Late*, 28.

41. Schulze, "Everything You Need to Know."

42. Neil Postman, *Technopoly: The Surrender of Culture to Technology* (New York: Knopf, 1992).

43. Ibid., xii.

CHAPTER 5: THE MEDIUM IS THE MASSAGE

1. Malcolm Muggeridge, *Christ and the Media* (Grand Rapids: Eerdmans, 1978), 70.

2. Marshall McLuhan, *Understanding Media: The Extensions of Man*, critical edition, ed. W. Terrence Gordon (1964; Corte Madera, CA: Gingko Press, 1994).

3. Marshall McLuhan and Quentin Fiore, *The Medium Is the Massage: An Inventory of Effects* (1967; Corte Madera, CA: Gingko Press, 2001), 26.

4. McLuhan, *Understanding Media*, 18.

5. Ibid., 31.

6. Ibid., xvi–xvii, 38–50.

7. Neil Postman, *Amusing Ourselves to Death* (New York: Penguin, 1985), 8.

8. Ibid., 9.

9. Ibid., 61.

10. Todd Gitlin, *Media Unlimited: How the Torrent of Images and Sounds Overwhelms Our Lives* (New York: Metropolitan Books, 2001), 6.

11. Ibid., 94.

12. Ibid., 3–4.

NOTES

13. Nicholas Carr, *The Shallows: What the Internet Is Doing to Our Brains* (New York: Norton, 2010), 3.

14. Ibid., 44.

15. Ibid., 116.

16. Ashley Wehrli, "Nine Hours of Screen Time Is the Norm for Kids Nowadays," *Moms*, July 25, 2021, www.moms.com/9-hours-screen-time-kids-pandemic/.

17. Sarah Knapton, "Social Media Damages Teen Mental Health through Cyberbullying, Sleep Loss and Too Little Exercise," *Telegraph*, August 13, 2019, www.telegraph.co.uk/science/2019/08/13/social-media-damages-teen-mental-health-cyberbullying-sleep/.

18. Study Finds, "Children's Screen Time Doubled during Pandemic—and Hasn't Changed Much Since," *Study Finds*, November 1, 2021, www.studyfinds.org/childrens-screen-time-doubled/.

19. "How Generation Porn Got Turned Off Sex," May 14, 2022, *Times*, www.thetimes.co.uk/article/how-generation-porn-got-turned-off-sex-rt9cwsrf8.

20. India Knight, "Porn Survey 2019: How Internet Pornography Is Changing the Way We Have Sex," *Times*, August 11, 2019, www.thetimes.co.uk/magazine/the-sunday-times-magazine/porn-survey-2019-how-internet-pornography-is-changing-the-way-we-have-sex-9qsg6n8kv.

21. Reuters, "Billie Eilish Says Watching Porn as a Child 'Destroyed My Brain,'" *Guardian*, December 14, 2021, www.theguardian.com/music/2021/dec/15/billie-eilish-says-watching-porn-gave-her-nightmares-and-destroyed-my-brain.

22. Derek Thompson, "Why Online Dating Can Feel Like Such an Existential Nightmare," *Atlantic*, July 21, 2019, www.theatlantic.com/ideas/archive/2019/07/online-dating-taking-over-everything/594337/.

23. Ibid.

24. Scott Hensley, "Poll: Americans Say We're Angrier Than a Generation Ago," NPR, June 26, 2019, www.npr.org/sections/health-shots/2019/06/26/735757156/poll-americans-say-were-angrier-than-a-generation-ago.

25. Nicholas Confessore, "How Tucker Carlson Reshaped Fox News," *New York Times*, April 30, 2022, www.nytimes.com/2022/04/30/us/tucker-carlson-fox-news.html.

26. Samantha Schmidt, "Americans' Views Flipped on Gay Rights. How Did Minds Change So Quickly?" *Washington Post*, June 7, 2019, www.washingtonpost.com/local/social-issues/americans-views-flipped-on-gay-rights-how-did-minds-change-so-quickly/2019/06/07/ae256016-8720-11e9-98c1-e945ae5db8fb_story.html.

27. Wikipedia, s.v. "Luddite," https://en.wikipedia.org/wiki/Luddite.

28. Jaron Lanier, *Ten Arguments for Deleting Your Social Media Accounts Right Now* (New York: Picador/Henry Holt, 2018), 125.

CHAPTER 6: UNAVOIDABLE TENSION

1. Overheard by Malcolm Muggeridge, quoted in his *Christ and the Media* (Grand Rapids: Eerdmans, 1978), 49.

2. Felicia Wu Song, *Restless Devices: Recovering Personhood, Presence, and Place in the Digital Age* (Downers Grove, IL: Intervarsity Academic, 2021), 9.

3. Heather Kelly and Emily Guskin, "Americans Widely Distrust Facebook, TikTok and Instagram with Their Data, Poll Finds," *Washington Post*, December 22, 2021, www.washingtonpost.com/technology/2021/12/22/tech-trust-survey/.

4. Nicholas Carr, *The Shallows: What the Internet Is Doing to Our Brains* (New York: Norton, 2010), 157.

5. Song, *Restless Devices*, 105.

6. Bonnie Kristian, "Why Church Shouldn't Just Be on Facebook," *Christianity Today*, October 6, 2021, www.christianitytoday.com/ct/2021/october-web-only/social-media-attention-church-shouldnt-just-be-on-facebook.html.

7. Kyuboem Lee, "How Might the COVID-19 Crisis Reshape Our Churches for Good?" *Christianity Today*, September 28, 2021, www.christianitytoday.com/pastors/2021/fall/how-might-covid-19-crisis-reshape-our-churches-for-good.html.

8. Jay Y. Kim, *Analog Church: Why We Need Real People, Places, and Things in the Digital Age* (Downers Grove, IL: Intervarsity, 2020).

9. Todd Gitlin, *Media Unlimited: How the Torrent of Images and Sounds Overwhelms Our Lives* (New York: Metropolitan Books, 2001), 210.

10. Tim Challies, *The Next Story: Life and Faith after the Digital Explosion* (Grand Rapids: Zondervan, 2011), 17.

11. Alan Noble, *Disruptive Witness: Speaking Truth in a Distracted Age*

(Downers Grove, IL: Intervarsity, 2018), 125. It should be noted that while I like these four questions, much of this book takes a dissenting view from Noble's own suggestions regarding the use of technology in the life of the church.

12. Millard Erickson, *Christian Theology*, 2nd ed. (Grand Rapids: Baker, 1983), 123–29.

13. For a further exploration of this, see James Emery White, *Meet Generation Z: Understanding and Reaching the New Post-Christian World* (Grand Rapids: Baker, 2017), 89–103.

14. The earliest reference to the designation that I am aware of is in a second-century letter to a Roman official named Diognetus.

15. Gerald L. Sittser, "The Early Church Thrived amid Secularism and Shows How We Can, Too," *Christianity Today*, October 16, 2019, www.christianitytoday.com/ct/2019/october-web-only/early-church-thrived-amid-secularism-we-can-too.html.

16. John R. W. Stott, *Christian Counter-Culture: The Message of the Sermon on the Mount* (Downers Grove, IL: Intervarsity, 1978).

17. Ibid., 65.

18. Muggeridge, *Christ and the Media*, 49.

19. Ibid.

20. Martin E. Marty, *A Short History of Christianity*, 2nd ed. (Philadelphia: Fortress, 1987), 169.

21. Bill J. Leonard, *Word of God across the Ages* (Nashville: Broadman, 1981), 38.

22. Tom Gjelten, "How Technology Helped Martin Luther Change Christianity," NPR, November 20, 2016, www.npr.org/2016/11/20/502437123/how-technology-helped-martin-luther-change-christianity.

23. Thomas Friedman, *Thank You for Being Late: An Optimist's Guide to Thriving in the Age of Accelerations* (New York: Farrar, Straus, and Giroux, 2016), 339. Obviously God is there but wants his people to join him as conveyors of his message.

INTERLUDE

1. Andrew M. Eason and Roger J. Green, eds. *Settled Views: The Shorter Writings of Catherine Booth* (Lanham: Lexington Books, 2017), 241.

2. On this, see the work of sociologist Rodney Stark, *The Rise of*

Christianity: How the Obsure, Marginal Jesus Movement Became the Dominant Religious Force in the Western World in a Few Centuries (San Francisco: HarperSanFrancisco, 1997).

3. Perhaps made most popular among Christians by George Barna and his book *The Frog and the Kettle: What Christians Need to Know about Life in the Year 2000* (Ventura, CA: Regal, 1990).

CHAPTER 7: OPENING THE DIGITAL FRONT DOOR

1. Carey Nieuwhof, "Three Shocking Statistics That Show How Quickly, Radically (and Permanently?) Church Has Changed Since 2020," *Carey Nieuwhof,* accessed October 26, 2020, https://careynieuwhof.com/3 -statistics-that-show-how-quickly-radically-and-permanently-church-is -changing-in-2020.

2. Kate Mabus, "Online or In-Person? Gen Z and Millennials Find Digital Life More Memorable, Study Shows," *USA Today*, July 1, 2021, www .usatoday.com/story/news/nation/2021/07/01/generation-z-millennial -survey-shows-digital-life-more-memorable/7783597002/.

3. Nieuwhof, "Three Shocking Statistics."

4. Kevin McSpadden, "You Now Have a Shorter Attention Span Than a Goldfish," *Time*, May 14, 2015, https://time.com/3858309/attention -spans-goldfish/.

5. Ashley Viens, "This Graph Tells Us Who's Using Social Media the Most," World Economic Forum, October 2, 2019, www.weforum.org /agenda/2019/10/social-media-use-by-generation/.

6. Alexandra Steigrad, "TikTok Overtakes Google as Most Popular Site in 2021," *New York Post*, December 23, 2021, https://nypost.com/2021 /12/23/tiktok-overtakes-google-as-most-popular-site-in-2021/.

7. Emma Bazilian, "Infographic: 50% of Gen Z 'Can't Live without YouTube' and Other Stats That Will Make You Feel Old," *Adweek*, May 21, 2017, www.adweek.com/performance-marketing/infographic -50-of-gen-z-cant-live-without-youtube-and-other-stats-that-will-make -you-feel-old/.

8. Jacob Dirnhuber, "Children Turn Backs on Traditional Careers in Favour of Internet Fame, Study Finds," *Sun*, May 22, 2017, www.thesun .co.uk/news/3617062/children-turn-backs-on-traditional-careers-in -favour-of-internet-fame-study-finds/.

9. Tanith Carey, "Can Social Media School Make Your Sixteen-Year-Old a

Star?" *Telegraph*, October 25, 2018, www.telegraph.co.uk/family /schooling/can-social-media-school-make-16-year-old-star/.

10. There are multiple issues related to copyrights and the use of YouTube videos. Some have no copyright issues at all and are free to use, others are quite strict. So do your due diligence before using one.

11. Brett Molina, "Baby Shark Is the First YouTube Video to Cross Ten Billion Views," *USA Today*, January 14, 2022, www.usatoday.com /story/tech/2022/01/14/baby-shark-youtube-10-billion-views /6524167001/.

12. Brandon Doyle, "TikTok Statistics—Updated August 2022," *Wallaroo Media*, August 13, 2022, https://wallaroomedia.com/blog/social-media /tiktok-statistics.

13. Rachel Seo, "Meet the TikTok Generation of Televangelists," *Christianity Today*, October 20, 2020, www.christianitytoday.com /ct/2020/november/meet-tik-tok-generation-z-televangelists-seo.html.

14. Aaron Earls, "Online Services Expanded Reach of Churches during Pandemic," *Outreach*, December 22, 2021, https://outreachmagazine. com/resources/research-and-trends/69988-online-services-expanded -reach-of-churches-during-pandemic.html.

15. Dave Adamson, "Church as We Know It Is Over. Here's What's Next," Fox News, March 11, 2019, www.foxnews.com/opinion/churches-as-we -know-it-are-over-here-is-how-to-engage-the-faithful.

16. "State of the Bible: USA 2021," American Bible Society, https://sotb .research.bible/.

17. Adelle M. Banks, "Amid COVID-19, Most Churches Provide Hybrid Worship, Half Stopped Picnics," Religion News Service, November 10, 2021, https://religionnews.com/2021/11/10/amid-covid-19-most -churches-provide-hybrid-worship-half-stopped-picnics/.

18. Carey Nieuwhof, "Twelve Disruptive Church Trends That Will Rule 2022 (and the Post-Pandemic Era)," *Carey Nieuwhof*, accessed January 3, 2022, https://careynieuwhof.com/12-disruptive-church-trends-that -will-rule-2022-and-the-post-pandemic-era.

19. Sarah Perez, "COVID-19 Pandemic Accelerated Shift to E-Commerce by Five Years, New Report Says," TechCrunch, August 24, 2020, https:// techcrunch.com/2020/08/24/covid-19-pandemic-accelerated-shift-to-e -commerce-by-5-years-new-report-says.

20. Adamson, "Church as We Know It Is Over."

CHAPTER 8: PLANTING ONLINE

1. Wikipedia, s.v. "Where No Man Has Gone Before," https://en.wikipedia.org/wiki/Where_no_man_has_gone_before.

2. Mecklenburg Community Church partners with Church and Culture to offer the annual Fall Church and Culture Conference, as well as a set of Spring Ministry Workshops. For more information, visit churchandculture.org.

3. Transcript, session 4, 2021 Church and Culture Conference, Mecklenburg Community Church.

4. Barna Group (@BarnaGroup), Twitter, April 5, 2021, 10:19 a.m., https://shop.barna.com/collections/state-of-digital-church.

5. Michael Gryboski, "Pastor John MacArthur Rejects Online Worship, Says Zoom Is 'Not Church,'" *Christian Post*, November 11, 2021, www.christianpost.com/news/pastor-john-macarthur-rejects-online-worship-its-not-church.html.

6. David Croteau, *Urban Legends of the New Testament: Forty Common Misconceptions* (Nashville: B&H Academic, 2015), 205–10.

7. Carey Nieuwhof, "The False Debate between Online and In-Person Church (How to Plan for an Uncertain Future)," *Carey Nieuwhof*, accessed March 7, 2021, https://careynieuwhof.com/the-false-debate-between-online-and-in-person-church-how-to-plan-for-an-uncertain-future/.

8. We offer separate content for children, on demand, sent out by email with links, as well as on our app.

9. Transcript, session 4, 2021 Church and Culture Conference, Mecklenburg Community Church.

10. Jonathan Sprowl, "Ministry in the Metaverse," *Outreach*, November 23, 2021, https://outreachmagazine.com/features/leadership/69751-ministry-in-the-metaverse.html.

11. David Roach, "The Next Mission Field Is a Game," *Christianity Today*, September 21, 2020, www.christianitytoday.com/ct/2020/october/esports-evangelism-gaming-ministry-coronavirus.html.

12. Jason Mitchell, "Getting the Metaverse Right—Can the Lessons of Social Marketing Guide Brands?" *AdAge*, January 6, 2022, https://adage.com/article/opinion/getting-metaverse-right-can-lessons-social-marketing-guide-brands/2391046.

13. Sprowl, "Ministry in the Metaverse."

14. Sarah Einselen, "Life Church Adds One More Site—In Virtual Reality," *Roys Report*, December 21, 2021, https://julieroys.com/life-church -multi-site-megachurch-virtual-reality/.
15. Sprowl, "Ministry in the Metaverse."
16. Ibid.
17. Chris Moon, "NewThing Hoping to Plant Hundreds of Digital Churches," *Christian Standard*, March 4, 2022, https:// christianstandard.com/2022/03/newthing-hoping-to-plant-hundreds-of -digital-churches/?utm_source=CT+Daily+Briefing+Newsletter&utm _medium=Newsletter&utm_term=224594&utm_content=8642&utm _campaign=email.
18. Corrina Laughlin, "Why Evangelicals Are Early Adopters of New Tech," *Atlantic*, December 21, 2021, www.theatlantic.com/ideas/archive/2021 /12/christmas-metaverse/621075.
19. Ibid.

CHAPTER 9: RETHINKING DELIVERY

1. Zee, "Newsweek in 1995: Why the Internet Will Fail," *Next Web*, February 27, 2010, https://thenextweb.com/news/newsweek-1995 -buy-books-newspapers-straight-intenet-uh.
2. Christopher Mims, "The Six Laws of Technology Everyone Should Know," *Wall Street Journal*, November 26, 2017, www.wsj.com/articles /the-6-laws-of-technology-everyone-should-know-1511701201.
3. Ibid.
4. Sarah Perez, "COVID-19 Pandemic Accelerated Shift to E-Commerce by Five Years, New Report Says," TechCrunch, August 24, 2020, https:// techcrunch.com/2020/08/24/covid-19-pandemic-accelerated-shift-to-e -commerce-by-5-years-new-report-says/.
5. Georgia Wells, "How People Can Make Smarter—and Healthier— Social-Media Choices," *Wall Street Journal*, December 13, 2021, www .wsj.com/articles/smarter-healthier-social-media-choices-11639177212.
6. Emily Sullivan, "Best Buy to Pull CDs from Its Stores, according to Report," NPR, February 6, 2018, www.npr.org/sections/thetwo-way /2018/02/06/583666258/best-buy-to-pull-cds-from-its-stores-according -to-report.
7. Stephanie Morgan, "Why Digital? What Digital Learning Can Bring

to Your Organisation," *Training Journal*, July 12, 2019, www
.trainingjournal.com/articles/features/why-digital-what-digital-learning
-can-bring-your-organisation.

8. Eli Zimmerman, "Four New Models of Higher Education for the Twenty-First Century," *EdTech*, July 3, 2019, https://edtechmagazine .com/higher/article/2019/07/4-models-reinvent-higher-education -21st-century.

9. Ibid.

10. Eli Zimmerman, "Higher Education Leaders and Students Explore AI-Enabled Video Platform [#Infographic]," *EdTech*, November 6, 2018, https://edtechmagazine.com/higher/article/2018/11/higher-education -leaders-and-students-explore-ai-enabled-video-platform-infographic.

11. Zimmerman, "Four New Models of Higher Education."

12. Ibid.

13. Laura Pappano, "The iGen Shift: Colleges Are Changing to Reach the Next Generation," *New York Times*, August 2, 2018, www.nytimes.com /2018/08/02/education/learning/generationz-igen-students-colleges .html; see also Corey Seemiller and Meghan Grace, *Generation Z Goes to College* (San Francisco: Jossey-Bass, 2016), and "Beyond Millennials: The Next Generation of Learners" (report), Pearson, August 2018, www .pearson.com/content/dam/one-dot-com/one-dot-com/global/Files /news/news-annoucements/2018/The-Next-Generation-of-Learners _final.pdf.

14. Ibid.

15. Ibid.

16. Ibid.

17. Stephanie Morgan, "Why Digital? What Digital Learning Can Bring to Your Organization," https://www.trainingjournal.com/articles/features /why-digital-what-digital-learning-can-bring-your-organisation

18. Ibid.

CHAPTER 10: IT'S A LONELY WORLD

1. Source unknown, but widely attributed to Mother Teresa.

2. Bethany Minelle, "Mark Zuckerberg: Facebook Can Be Your Church," *Sky News*, June 28, 2017, https://news.sky.com/story/mark-zuckerberg -facebook-can-be-your-church-10929518.

3. Halee Gray Scott, "The Gospel of Mark Zuckerberg," *Christianity Today*, August 10, 2017, www.christianitytoday.com/ct/2017/august -web-only/gospel-of-mark-zuckerberg.html.

4. Ibid.

5. Dennis Green, "Gen Z Says Everyone Has an iPhone These Days—and If They Don't, They Get Left Out of Group Chats," *Business Insider*, July 1, 2019, www.businessinsider.com/gen-z-iphone-ownership-creates -culture-of-multitasking-2019-6.

6. Elizabeth A. Segal, PhD, "Metaverse Is the Wrong Solution to the Right Problem," *Psychology Today*, October 29, 2021, www.psychologytoday .com/us/blog/social-empathy/202110/metaverse-is-the-wrong-solution -the-right-problem.

7. "Cigna's U.S. Loneliness Index: Survey of 20,000 Americans Examining Behaviors Driving Loneliness in the United States," Cigna, May 1, 2018, www.multivu.com/players/English/8294451-cigna-us-loneliness-survey; see also Jayne O'Donnell and Shari Rudavsky, "Young Americans Are the Loneliest, Surprising Study from Cigna Shows," *USA Today*, May 1, 2018, www.usatoday.com/story/news/politics/2018/05/01/loneliness -poor-health-reported-far-more-among-young-people-than-even-those -over-72/559961002/; and Jamie Ducharme, "Young Americans Are the Loneliest, according to a New Study," *Time*, May 1, 2018, https://time .com/5261181/young-americans-are-lonely/.

8. Jean M. Twenge, *iGen: Why Today's Super-Connected Kids Are Growing Up Less Rebellious, More Tolerant, Less Happy—and Completely Unprepared for Adulthood* (New York: Atria, 2017), 71.

9. Brian Resnick, "Twenty-Two Percent of Millennials Say They Have 'No Friends,'" *Vox*, August 1, 2019, www.vox.com/science-and-health/2019 /8/1/20750047/millennials-poll-loneliness.

10. Robert Putnam, *Bowling Alone: The Collapse and Revival of American Community* (New York: Simon and Schuster, 2000).

11. Jean Bethke Elshtain, foreword to *Habits of the High-Tech Heart*, by Quentin J. Schultze (Grand Rapids: Baker Academic, 2002), 10.

12. Sherry Turkle, *Alone Together: Why We Expect More from Technology and Less from Each Other* (New York: Basic Books, 2011), 11.

13. Ibid., 155.

14. Ibid., 295.

15. Felicia Wu Song, *Restless Devices: Recovering Personhood, Presence, and*

Place in the Digital Age (Downers Grove, IL: Intervarsity Academic, 2021), 108.

16. Megan Fowler, "In Christ, Alone: Most Believers Say They Don't Need Others for Discipleship," *Christianity Today*, August 22, 2019, www.christianitytoday.com/news/2019/august/lifeway-discipleship -assessment-growth-alone.html.

17. Yuval Noah Harari, *Twenty-One Lessons for the Twenty-First Century* (New York: Spiegel and Grau, 2018), 88–89.

18. Transcript, Session Four, 2021 Church and Culture Conference, Mecklenburg Community Church.

19. "State of the Bible: USA 2021," American Bible Society, https://sotb .research.bible/.

20. Elizabeth Dias, "Facebook's Next Target: The Religious Experience," *New York Times*, July 25, 2021, www.nytimes.com/2021/07/25/us /facebook-church.html.

21. Ibid.

CHAPTER 11: REVISIONING COMMUNITY

1. Dietrich Bonhoeffer, *Life Together*, trans. John W. Doberstein (New York: HarperSanFrancisco, 1954), 20.

2. Betsy Morris, "Most Teens Prefer to Chat Online, Rather Than In Person," *Wall Street Journal*, September 10, 2018, www.wsj.com/articles /most-teens-prefer-to-chat-online-than-in-person-survey-finds -1536597971. See also Laura Pappano, "The iGen Shift: Colleges Are Changing to Reach the Next Generation," *New York Times*, August 2, 2018, www.nytimes.com/2018/08/02/education/learning/generationz -igen-students-colleges.html; and "Beyond Millennials: The Next Generation of Learners" (report), Pearson, August 2018, www.pearson .com/content/dam/one-dot-com/one-dot-com/global/Files/news/news -annoucements/2018/The-Next-Generation-of-Learners_final.pdf.

3. Kate Mabus, "Online or In Person? Gen Z and Millennials Find Digital Life More Memorable, Study Shows," *USA Today*, July 1, 2021, www .usatoday.com/story/news/nation/2021/07/01/generation-z-millennial -survey-shows-digital-life-more-memorable/7783597002/.

4. Diana Aguilera, "The Truth about Online Lying," *Stanford Magazine*, September 2018, https://stanfordmag.org/contents/the-truth-about -online-lying.

5. "Seven Shifts Churches Need to Make because of the Coronavirus—Episode 142: The Unstuck Church Podcast," *Tony Morgan Live*, April 22, 2020, https://tonymorganlive.com/2020/04/22/7-shifts-churches-need-to-make-because-of-coronavirus-episode-142-unstuck-church-podcast/.

6. Stephen Lowe, "With All Your Heart, Soul, Wi-Fi, and Websites," interview by Mark Galli, *Christianity Today*, April 22, 2019, www.christianitytoday.com/ct/2019/may/stephen-mary-lowe-ecologies-faith-digital-age.html.

7. Emily Drooby, "Gen. Z Is Replacing Face-to-Face Hanging Out with 'Live Chilling,'" *USA Today/Buzz60*, February 20, 2017, www.usatoday.com/videos/news/2017/02/20/gen.-z-replacing-face-face-hanging-out-'live-chilling'/98152098/.

8. Sarah Perez, "Houseparty Reports 50M Sign-Ups in Past Month amid COVID-19 Lockdowns," TechCrunch, April 15, 2020, https://techcrunch.com/2020/04/15/houseparty-reports-50m-sign-ups-in-past-month-amid-covid-19-lockdowns/.

9. Deep Patel, "Twelve Social Media Trends to Watch in 2020," *Entrepreneur*, December 20, 2019, https://www.entrepreneur.com/article/343863.

10. Andrew Hutchinson, "New Study Shows That Text Messaging Is the Most Popular Form of Digital Interaction in Emerging Markets," *Social Media Today*, August 27, 2019, www.socialmediatoday.com/news/new-study-shows-that-text-messaging-is-the-most-popular-form-of-digital-int/561709/.

11. "Why Messaging Businesses Is the New Normal," *Meta for Business*, June 14, 2018, www.facebook.com/business/news/insights/why-messaging-businesses-is-the-new-normal.

12. Marianne Walker, "Social Media Trends and Stats for 2020," *Virginia Media*, June 4, 2020, www.virginiamedia.com/blog/social-media-trends-and-stats-for-2020/.

13. Ibid.

14. Ibid.

CHAPTER 12: ONLINE CAMPUS COMMUNITY

1. C. T. Casberg, "The Surprising Theological Possibilities of Virtual Reality," *Christianity Today*, November 11, 2016, www.christianitytoday

.com/ct/2016/november-web-only/surprising-theological-possibilities
-of-virtual-reality.html.

2. Bob Smietana, "Online Communion Should Be Celebrated, Not Shunned, Says Diana Butler Bass," Religion News Service, May 15, 2020, https://religionnews.com/2020/05/15/online-communion-should-be -celebrated-not-shunned-says-diana-butler-bass/.

3. Adelle Banks, "Virtual Bathtub Baptisms Help Maryland Megachurch Gain Members during Pandemic," *Roys Report*, April 16, 2022, https:// julieroys.com/virtual-bathtub-baptisms-church-gain-members-during -pandemic/.

4. E. F. Schumacher, *Small Is Beautiful: Economics As If People Mattered* (New York: Harper and Row, 1973).

CHAPTER 13: THE MISSION

1. Lesslie Newbigin, *Foolishness to the Greeks: The Gospel and Western Culture* (Grand Rapids: Eerdmans, 1986), 1.

2. Kate Shellnutt, "Southern Baptist Church Planting Up in 2020, but Baptisms Plunge by Half," *Christianity Today*, May 21, 2021, www .christianitytoday.com/news/2021/may/southern-baptist-decline-covid -annual-church-profile-sbc.html.

3. Aaron Earls, "The Church Growth Gap: The Big Get Bigger while the Small Get Smaller," *Christianity Today*, March 6, 2019, www .christianitytoday.com/news/2019/march/lifeway-research-church -growth-attendance-size.html.

4. Yonat Shimron, "Study: Attendance Hemorrhaging at Small and Midsize US Congregations," Religion News Service, October 14, 2021, https://religionnews.com/2021/10/14/study-attendance-at-small-and -midsize-us-congregations-is-hemorrhaging/; Adam MacInnis, "Evangelism Not a Priority in Canadian Churches," *Christianity Today*, October 13, 2021, www.christianitytoday.com/news/2021/october /canada-evangelism-church-study.html.

5. Steve Cable, "Introducing Probe's New Survey: Religious Views and Practices 2020," *Probe for Answers*, June 30, 2021, https://probe .org/article-introducing-probes-new-survey-religious-views-and -practices-2020/. See also Leonardo Blair, "Nearly 70% of Born -Again Christians Say Other Religions Can Lead to Heaven: Study," *Christian Post*, October 21, 2021, www.christianpost.com/news

/nearly-70-percent-of-born-again-christians-dont-see-jesus-as-only
-way.html.

6. "Americans Express Increasingly Warm Feelings toward Religious
Groups," Pew Research Center, February 15, 2017, www.pewforum
.org/2017/02/15/americans-express-increasingly-warm-feelings-toward
-religious-groups/; Kate Shellnutt, "Americans Warm Up to Every
Religious Group Except Evangelicals," *Christianity Today*, February 15,
2017, www.christianitytoday.com/news/2017/february/americans
-warm-feelings-religious-groups-evangelicals-pew.html.

7. Lesslie Newbigin, *The Gospel in a Pluralist Society* (Grand Rapids:
Eerdmans, 1989), 141.

8. Catherine Turner, "In an 'Infobesity' Age Researchers Must Innovate
to Ensure Senior Interest and Buy-In," *Research Live*, March 14, 2019,
www.research-live.com/article/news/in-the-age-of-infobesity
-researchers-must-innovate-to-ensure-senior-interest-and-buyin/id
/5051102.

CHAPTER 14: REACHING OUT ONLINE

1. Ashley Viens, "This Graph Tells Us Who's Using Social Media the
Most," World Economic Forum, October 2, 2019, www.weforum.org
/agenda/2019/10/social-media-use-by-generation/.

2. Philip Kotler with Hermawan Kartajaya and Iwan Setiawan, *Marketing
4.0: Moving from Traditional to Digital* (Hoboken, NJ: John Wiley, 2017).

3. "Will Making Religion Social Media-Friendly Win Over Gen Z and
Millennials?" *YPulse*, October 23, 2019, www.ypulse.com/article/2019
/10/23/will-making-religion-social-media-friendly-win-over-gen-z-
millennials/.

4. Rick Richardson, *You Found Me: New Research on How Unchurched
Nones, Millennials, and Irreligious Are Surprisingly Open to Christian
Faith* (Downers Grove, IL: Intervarsity, 2019), 65–66.

5. Khadeeja Safdar, "Churches Target New Members, with Help from Big
Data," *Wall Street Journal*, December 26, 2021, www.wsj.com/articles
/churches-new-members-personal-online-data-analytics-gloo
-11640310982.

6. Ibid.

7. On opening the physical front door, see James Emery White, *Rethinking
the Church* (1997; Grand Rapids: Baker, 2003); White, *What They Didn't*

Teach You in Seminary (Grand Rapids: Baker, 2011); and White, *The Rise of the Nones* (Grand Rapids: Baker, 2014). And if you can find a copy, White, *Opening the Front Door* (Nashville: Convention Press, 1992).

8. Elizabeth Schulze, "Everything You Need to Know about the Fourth Industrial Revolution," CNBC, January 17, 2019, www.cnbc.com /2019/01/16/fourth-industrial-revolution-explained-davos-2019.html.

9. Eben Esterhuizen, "Phygital: Six Ways to Adapt, or Die," *Bizcommunity*, April 30, 2019, www.bizcommunity.com/Article/196/458/190287.html.

10. Mike Welsh, "The Future Is Phygital: Physical and Digital," *Mobiquity*, April 19, 2021, www.mobiquity.com/insights/the-future-is-phygital.

11. "Gen Z Goes Phys-igtal," PYMNTS.com, April 25, 2017, www.pymnts .com/data-drivers/2017/gen-z-goes-phys-igtal-sandeep-bhanote-radius8 -bricks-and-mortar-ecommerce-consumer-insights/.

12. Mike Murphy, "Apple Wants Kids to Hang Out at Apple Stores," *Quartz*, April 25, 2017, https://qz.com/968103/apple-aapl-retail-chief -angela-ahrendts-wants-generation-z-to-hang-out-at-apple-stores/.

13. Jim Kearney and Erik Steffensen, "Cutting the Branches: The Case for Letting Go of Physical Locations," BAI, March 14, 2019, www.bai.org /banking-strategies/article-detail/cutting-the-branches-the-case-for -letting-go-of-physical-locations/.

14. Critical Software, "The Phygital Touch: Fusing Digital and Physical in Finance," *FinTech*, November 5, 2020, https://fintechmagazine.com /banking/phygital-touch-fusing-digital-and-physical-finance.

15. Tiffany Hsu and Sapna Maheshwari, "'Thumb-Stopping,' 'Humaning,' 'B4H': The Strange Language of Modern Marketing," *New York Times*, November 5, 2020, www.nytimes.com/2020/11/25/business/media /thumb-stopping-humaning-b4h-the-strange-language-of-modern -marketing.html.

16. Esterhuizen, "Phygital."

17. Schulze, "Everything You Need to Know."

18. Corrina Laughlin, *Redeem All: How Digital Life is Changing Evangelical Culture* (Oakland: Univ. of California Press, 2022), 42.

19. Scott Wassmer, "A Look into Four of the Top Digital Trends for 2022," Drum, December 2, 2021, www.thedrum.com/opinion/2021/12/02 /look-four-the-top-digital-trends-2022.

20. "Mobile Fact Sheet," Pew Research Center, April 7, 2021, www.pew research.org/internet/fact-sheet/mobile/.

21. Chris Williams, "Americans Check Their Smartphones Ninety-Six Times a Day, Survey Says," Fox 13 Seattle, September 28, 2021, www .q13fox.com/news/americans-check-their-smartphones-96-times-a -day-survey-says.

22. Sam Haysom, "People Spend a Third of Their Waking Day Staring at Their Phones, Report Finds," *Mashable*, January 12, 2022, https:// mashable.com/article/mobile-phone-app-use-report.

23. "The Church App," Subsplash, https://www.thechurchapp.org/.

24. Dale Chamberlain, "YouVersion Bible App Hits 500 Million Installs," *ChurchLeaders*, November 10, 2021, https://churchleaders.com/news /410006-youversion-bible-app-hits-500-million-installs.html.

25. Bobby Guenewald, "Q&A with YouVersion Founder Bobby Gruenewald," interview by Craig Groeschel, YouTube video, posted by Craig Groeschel Leadership Podcast on August 1, 2018, www.youtube .com/watch?v=1fxPn1JVyks. Quote appears at the 4:00 mark.

26. "YouVersion Is Celebrating 500 Million Installs!" *YouVersion*, November 10, 2021, https://blog.youversion.com/2021/11/youversion -is-celebrating-500-million-installs/.

27. "State of the Bible: USA 2021," American Bible Society, https://sotb .research.bible/.

CHAPTER 15: PROCESS AND EVENT

1. Lewis Carroll, *Alice's Adventures in Wonderland* (New York: Knopf, 1984), 89.

2. Michael Green, *Evangelism in the Early Church* (London: Hodder and Stoughton, 1970), 173.

3. Rick Richardson, *You Found Me: New Research on How Unchurched Nones, Millennials, and Irreligious Are Surprisingly Open to Christian Faith* (Downers Grove, IL: Intervarsity, 2019), 58.

4. Ibid., 61–62.

5. Darrel Girardier, "Two Significant Shifts in the Trajectory of Social Media," *Outreach*, November 29, 2021, https://outreachmagazine.com /features/leadership/69774-few-pastors-left-the-pulpit-despite-pandemic -pressures.html.

6. Ellen Byron, "America's Retailers Have a New Target Customer: The Twenty-Six-Year-Old Millennial," *Wall Street Journal*, October 9, 2017,

www.wsj.com/articles/americas-retailers-have-a-new-target-customer
-the-26-year-old-millennial-1507559181.

7. Carey Nieuwhof, "Five Important Ways Evangelism Is Shifting in Our
Post-Christian World," *Carey Nieuwhof*, accessed April 20, 2015, https://
careynieuwhof.com/5-important-ways-evangelism-is-shifting-in-a-post
-christian-world/.

8. Ibid.

9. Dietrich Bonhoeffer, *The Cost of Discipleship* (New York: Macmillan, 1937).

CHAPTER 16: WHAT BUSINESS ARE YOU IN?

1. Fred R. Shapiro, ed., *The Yale Book of Quotations* (New Haven, CT: Yale
Univ. Press, 2006), 8.

2. Heather Kelly, "Things the iPhone Killed," CNN, June 29, 2017,
https://money.cnn.com/2017/06/29/technology/gadgets/things-the
-iphone-killed/index.html.

3. Doug Murren, *LeaderShift* (Ventura, CA: Regal, 1994), 70.

4. Steve Lohr and Carlos Tejada, "After Era That Made It a Verb, Xerox, in
a Sale, Is Past Tense," *New York Times*, January 31, 2018, www.nytimes
.com/2018/01/31/business/dealbook/xerox-fujifilm.html.

5. Ibid.

6. Dominic Walsh, "Hotels Offer Distracted Home Workers a Little
Privacy," *Times*, August 6, 2020, www.thetimes.co.uk/edition/business
/hotels-offer-distracted-home-workers-a-little-privacy-c5s6c8zc9.

7. Jeanne Whalen, "Struggling U.S. Manufacturers Pivot to One Product
Where Sales Are Actually Booming: Masks," *Washington Post*, August 5,
2020, www.washingtonpost.com/business/2020/08/05/face-masks
-made-usa.

8. Vanessa Romo, "Dunkin' Deletes Donuts from Its Name," NPR,
September 26, 2018, www.npr.org/2018/09/26/651905960/dunkin
-deletes-donuts-from-its-name.

9. Daniel Silliman, "Why Gideons International Is Scaling Back Bible
Printing," *Christianity Today*, March 17, 2020, www.christianitytoday
.com/ct/2020/april/gideons-bible-printer-closes-refocuses-rebalances
.html.

10. Jim Collins and Bill Lazier, *BE 2.0: Turning Your Business into an
Enduring Great Company* (New York: Penguin, 2020), 112.

NOTES

11. Jim Collins, *Turning the Flywheel: A Monograph to Accompany Good to Great* (New York: HarperCollins, 2019), 1.
12. Brad Stone, *The Everything Store: Jeff Bezos and the Age of Amazon* (New York: Hachette, 2013), quoted in Collins, *Turning the Flywheel*, 2.

CHAPTER 17: STRATEGY VERSUS TACTICS

1. Daniel Boorstin, *The Discoverers* (New York: Random House, 1983) xvi.
2. Carey Nieuwhof, "Five Disruptive Church Trends That Will Rule 2019," *Carey Nieuwhof*, accessed January 2, 2019, https://careynieuwhof.com/5-disruptive-church-trends-that-will-rule-2019/.
3. Justin Bariso, "IKEA Just Quietly Killed It's Famous Catalog. It's a Brilliant Lesson in Emotional Intelligence," *Inc.*, December 31, 2020, www.inc.com/justin-bariso/ikea-just-quietly-killed-its-famous-catalog-its-a-brilliant-lesson-in-emotional-intelligence.html.
4. "After Seventy Successful Years, IKEA Is Turning the Page on the Catalog," IKEA, December 7, 2020, https://about.ikea.com/en/newsroom/2020/12/07/after-70-successful-years-ikea-is-turning-the-page.
5. Adam Grant, *Think Again: The Power of Knowing What You Don't Know* (New York: Viking, 2021).

AFTERWORD

1. Eric Schmidt and Jared Cohen, *The New Digital Age: Reshaping the Future of People, Nations and Business* (New York: Knopf, 2013), opening epigraph.
2. John Longhurst, "Church of Canada May Disappear by 2040, Says New Report," Religion News Service, November 18, 2019, https://religionnews.com/2019/11/18/church-of-canada-may-disappear-by-2040-says-new-report/.
3. Ibid.
4. Ibid.

Explore
ChurchandCulture.org
BLOG | HEADLINE NEWS | RESOURCES

CHURCH&CULTURE   about   blog   **resources**   speaking engagements   contact   search

Messages by James Emery White

These are the sermon series delivered by James Emery White at Mecklenburg Community Church. For your convenience, you'll find them organized by category. Messages are available in .mp3 or .pdf formats; in the latter format you'll find the entire written manuscript including programming notes should you wish to develop a similar set of sermons.

Current Series:

CHURCH&CULTURE   about   blog   **resources**   speaking engagements   contact   search

Here's what's happening on the church and culture front today...

Amazon's Alexa could soon have opinions and make decisions for you

At Amazon's re:MARS conference in Las Vegas last week, Jeff Bezos unveiled a flurry of startling new technologies which offered a glimpse into the future the Seattle-based company is dreaming up for consumers (Boland, *The Telegraph*)

Read more>>

Jun 13, 2019

Sex-abuse allegations grow against Catholic clergy in Poland

The Catholic Church in Poland has seen an uptick in accusations from people claiming to have been sexually abused by clergy as children, after a YouTube video sparked public anger at an institution that is at the political and social heart of this culturally conservative country. (Hinshaw, *The Wall Street Journal*)

Read more>>

Jun 13, 2019

CHURCH&CULTURE   about   blog   **resources**   speaking engagements   contact   search

The Real Challenge of Millennial Giving

June 13, 2019

"Millennials want to give to a cause."

Heard that one? Of course you have. And it's true. Just not the whole truth.

Here's all of it:

EVERYBODY wants to give to a cause.

It's just Millennials who are holding the church accountable to having one (which, I might add, is a good thing). So how have many responded in a knee-jerk fashion? By creating "boutique" giving options that offer channeled, specific giving to direct "causes" that bypass the general operating budget of a church or nonprofit.

So instead of giving to a general operating budget that might result in, say, a desk or a laptop or a 401K for field workers (no "cause" there, right? Just that damnable, wicked, evil "overhead "), you can give to drilling a specific water well outside of Lusaka, Zambia that will serve 112 AIDS orphans.

Pure, unadulterated "cause" giving.

So quick, which one do you want to give to—the "overhead" desk or the water well?

And all God's people said, "Water well."

Here's the problem. That water well won't be dug without a desk. Meaning a person on the field, in that area, serving as a liaison between your money and the actual completion of digging that well. Not to mention identifying the AIDS orphans who will be served.

The desk IS the water well.

How do I know?

To carry our example out, I personally traveled to Lusaka, Zambia. Our church had just sponsored

Search Posts

🔍 Search

Post Archive ⌄

Subscribe

Sign up to receive the twice-weekly Church & Culture blog delivered straight to your email account

Email Address

SIGN UP

We respect your privacy. Please refer to our *Privacy Policy* for more information

Featured Posts

...ilize assisted

...on Wednesday, ...y ill people to end ... measure will allow ...t to terminally ill

...offered a glimpse

...ergy as children, ...ervative country.

...erscoring the ...g. (O'Donnell, *USA*